LOVERS' TRIALS

By Loretta Moore

Contents

Chapter One

Anita and Carol's parents Julia and Joshua Bernstein began a relationship in 1961, at an unstable time while both attended Temple University in Philadelphia. Julia Walker's roommate introduced Joshua Bernstein, a student senior, aimed for the medical profession and Julia Walker, a junior at the prestigious school by way of an academic scholarship, aimed for a degree in social work. Instantly, the couple knew they wanted to be together regardless of the difference in their race and background. They fell deeply in love and nothing could discourage them from pursuing life together.

From a struggling South Carolina family, Julia Walker Bernstein grew up with five siblings. The pretty, tall, brown skinned Julia and lanky, handsome Joshua Bernstein met on the Temple University campus in 1961. She'd come to the prestigious school through an academic scholarship.

"Joshua, what is this you're saying, that you have a Negro girlfriend? This is just not right for our family," Norma Bernstein strongly told her son, in opposition. Despite his mother's resistance, a couple of months later Julia Walker was welcomed at the prominent Bernstein family's home in upstate New York.

Julia and Joshua became engaged only months after they met, and married immediately. The couple did not have his parent's approval to marry and so went to the Justice of the Peace in Elkton, Maryland to make their vows to each other.

After Joshua and Julia Bernstein began life as a married couple they immediately joined a commune. Soon after the couple joined the commune in Philadelphia, the first daughter, Anita was born. A year and half later, daughter Carol came into the world.

America was ablaze with activism. The country was a hot bed of antiwar and civil right activism. A high number of young people participated in that unsettled atmosphere, many of them college and university students. During this calamitous time some dropped out of normal society for the communal lifestyle. Joshua and Julia Bernstein fell into that category. The Bernstein family landed in a number of communes across the nation.

Living on the fringe of society was not without its difficulties nevertheless, it was a lifestyle they preferred. As the family moved about, Anita and Carol never faced problems going from school to school for they were academically strong. However, always the attractive sisters confronted backlash from African American girls saying things such as: "you think you cute, don't you!"

For the most part communes supported through their own endeavors selling vegetables they grew, jewelry they made, and anything the group could produce and sell at highways stands, bazaars, and flea markets, and other such venues.

Despite the many out of the norm aspects the communal life posed, the sisters experienced a free floating component roving the atmosphere with magic, mystery and pleasure in the surroundings!

For certain, throughout the 1960's the country experimented with loose ideas; rebellion and civil unrest raged. The rules of normal behavior changed to a society all about serving 'self'; you heard the 'buzz' phrases, 'do your own thing,' 'it's your prerogative.' You saw everything 'breaking out' in American society!

Around the country, protesters filled spaces with signs and shouts against the Viet Nam War; "Say It Loud, I'm Black and I'm Proud."

"I can't believe we ever lived like that," Julia Bernstein laughingly once said to her **husband, Joshua. At this point, the two were in their nice, comfortable family room** watching a movie about the hippie era. Joshua Bernstein lovingly placed his hand on hers. "No doubt about it, the lifestyle change was better for our family."

As much as moving about with a group of young people presented wonderful mysteries and adventure, the parental role wasn't positioned properly. Parents would sometimes smoke so much pot and use other drugs that the older children had to look out for the younger ones in the commune. The children close as second cousins, witnessed much overwhelming unbecoming, unpleasant conduct going on in the anti-established, unrestrained, loose lifestyle.

"Look, you do what I want, or I'll slap the heck out of you," a thirteen-year-old red-haired boy named Charlie who lived in the commune threatened Anita. "Let me go, and I won't mention this. Just let me go," fear-stricken and crying, Anita begged.

"Okay, Anita, I'm sorry. I don't know what came over me. I guess I just lost it," he said, shaking his head as he released her. "Please, don't tell anyone about what just happened, please, I'm so sorry," he pleaded. She said she wouldn't, with his head down, he walked away.

Also a mal-intentioned stranger might slip into the commune posing danger to the children.

A lot that was going on in the commune made the sisters and other children feel they didn't have life as children in normal families. As united as the group appeared loop holes certainly existed, many instances when the children didn't have a parental eye on them. Unfortunately during those times some things that should not have happened that did. However, perhaps the same kinds of mishaps might have occurred with some families and people in normal general society.

****

The two sisters, Anita and Carol Bernstein didn't object, or hadn't been totally displeased about the rambling lifestyle they'd experienced, but they appreciated family life so much more after their parents decided to change matters by settling down. The girls had become pre-teens when their parents moved into their professions, he as a physician and she a social worker, when they took up living as a normal middle-class family.

Anita and Carol Bernstein were in their early teens when the family turned away from the wandering life they'd been living, and settled down in a nice Philadelphia community. With that move the world took on a whole new brighter meaning.

In the new settled lifestyle, Anita and Carol became easily became comfortable with schools. They particularly enjoyed becoming members of the 'dramatics club'. Acting turned out to be a natural fit for Anita and Carol. The sisters greatly enjoyed releasing themselves to a script, and acting before a theatre audience. Whatever the reason, the 'dramatics club' became home for Anita and Carol. The drama teacher offered the sisters major roles in marvelous productions. Having no idea about their daughters' talent, Julia and Joshua Bernstein didn't instantly accept the 'acting' thing. However, the girls' performances surprised them, and made them proud parents.

****

Most summers Julia Bernstein had sent Anita and Carol to spend time with their grandmother in Ambler, South Carolina. Beginning when the sisters were preteens they took a greyhound bus south every summer. Julia Smalls Bernstein treasured her southern background and wanted her daughters to know her mother and relatives, and taste some of the things she'd grown up with. Always, Anita and Carol ended up having an enjoyable time with their grandmother. It seemed everyone in the small all-Negro community opened their hearts to the girls. The simple country folk treated them incredibly. "Hey deah, how yall?" Grandma fixin' y'all some fried chicken and some fried cone, 'n' crowda peas." And the girls certainly enjoyed the countless admiring boys in the area.

"A 'Red Bone,' that's what you is, you, and yo' sister." Local blacks in Ambler, South Carolina gave the sisters the common southern label 'Red bone' because of their fair complexion. It is understandable that the girls received so much attention, for they were truly beautiful. Carol, still quite young, was pursued to a lesser degree when the family made their Ambler, South Carolina visits. "Can I take you to the café (kaa-fay, 'n' buy you a 'pop?" Or the girls were invited to a movie, which they referred to as, a 'show.' The girls would always remember their young admirers for their extreme kindness, their great respect, and the starched and iron shirts, and creased pants, and their 'juicy-fruit' chewing gum. It was always a sad time when they had to depart Ambler, South Carolina. However it was the boys in Ambler Anita and Carol had encountered who struggled hardest, their spirits were lowest, because the girls were leaving.

"Carol, don't tell me you have three letters and we haven't been home a week yet" not totally pleased, Julia asked her daughter Anita. Anita, here's two for you. Those boys might be 'country', but are too fast for me. Turning to her husband, "What do you think about that, Joshua? Already five boys have written our girls letters from Ambler?

By the time the family returned home, the girls were deluged with mail from their southern suitors. "You Know how I feel, I don't appreciate all that attention my daughters are getting.'" Disgustedly, reluctantly, she handed her daughter the letters.

"Anita began reading a letter. "Mama, Dad, can you believe this, this boy is proposing marriage!"

"You write that young man right back and tell him that you have at least ten years before you'll even start thinking about marriage!" Joshua Bernstein adamantly told his older daughter.

"If she won't, I will. Or better yet, I'll go to Ambler, South Carolina and personally tell that young man something. And, I know you don't want that, and he certainly won't," red-faced, he angrily added. Another aspect of Anita and Carol Bernstein involved the times they spent with the family of Aunt Evelyn, their mother's sister.

Anita always felt as though she was stepping into another world when she visited her Aunt Evelyn, her mother's sister, and her husband Barry and their three children. Her life became more exciting in the City. The lives of her Aunt Evelyn, Uncle Barry and three young cousins seemed packed with fun and activity.

"From the bottom of my heart, dear, I apologize…" Young Anita sang into microphone, pretending to be the famous smooth-singing balladeer, Billy Eckstein. Her Uncle Barry's fashionable nightclub/ restaurants put her in touch with a level of glamour and excitement. It seemed to Ginger at both classy locations, that many of the patrons were glamorous-most appeared to be people of elevated status, and even had star-quality. The interior of the clubs was so astounding that when she stepped inside, she imagined she was in some of the incredible, glamour filled nightclubs she'd seen in movies. Her Aunt Evelyn and Uncle Barry would take her cousins and her to the clubs, during the hours of daylight of course. The club was a glaringly extravagant, enormous place with many different rooms, barrooms, and restaurants. But the huge, elaborate main ballroom that was absolutely breath-taking: it had a high ornate ceiling, and intricately designed moldings on the tops of the walls, crystal chandeliers and glistening mirrors everywhere, and there were gleaming parquet flooring-the children enjoyed gliding in their stocking feet on the parquet floors. Once, when she was around thirteen years old when they visited the club in downtown Philadelphia, magic was spun for Anita and Carol and their three cousins. The handsome, talented balladeer/performer Billy Eckstein was in the ballroom rehearsing for a performance that night-as he vocalized with a five-piece band, the kitchen and janitorial staffs stopped what they were doing to come see him and hear his rich sound. Everyone was mesmerized. The famous singer spun magic for all of the young cousins as well.

Chapter Two

Eddie Ramsey hailed from that special group of upper-crust African American families principally in the Philadelphia area, known as the Black elite. The Ramsey family is financially successful and the lifestyle is progressive, glossy and elaborate- they appear to live on the wings of life.

Eddie Ramsey's father, Doctor Henry Ramsey, was a cardiologist at the Pennsylvania University Hospital, with a successful private practice as well. Delores Robinson Ramsey, Eddie's mother was a practicing psychologist. Eddie and Judy, his sister two years younger and parents comprised the Ramsey family (Dr. Henry Ramsey had attended Meharry Medical School in Memphis, Tennessee, and Delores his wife, gained her education at Spelman College in Atlanta, Georgia, and then at Temple University in Philadelphia for her post-graduate degrees).

The elevated Ramsey's were associated with everything symbolic of upper class African Americans. (Almost unanimously they put their children in an exclusive organization called "Jack and Jill." Their children went to private schools; the women belonged to a social groups, the most prominent of all called, "Girl Friends'; the men were members of an exclusive professional fraternal organization called 'The Boule'. Many of the families attended the Episcopal or Congregational Church; they had summer homes on Martha's Vineyard, The Hamptons, Long Island, and Highland Beach. Speaking of Highland Beach located in Annapolis, Maryland, this is the favorite playground of the Ramsey's and those associated with the family).

The Ramsey's adhered to the strict requirements black upper-class families very often embrace. Everyone in the group had fair complexions, straight or wavy hair texture, delicate features and light eye color. They were also exclusive when it came to their professions and status, and they centered their lives on money, prestige, elevation, virtues and nobility.

The Ramsey family's impressive house was a lovely large Tudor tucked in a section outside of Philadelphia. It was a setting with an atmosphere that linked the lush, inviting surroundings with 'Age of Enlightenment' or the Renaissance period. The Ramseys' were perched high in society. Nonetheless, as with all Blacks back then, the high-level Ramsey's experienced rejection, restrictions and prejudice. (During the 1940'50's 60's, and 70's a group of activists Blacks under the auspices of Roy Wilkins, Adam Clayton Powell, and Thurgood Marshall tried to strangle the harsh reality of racial injustice. Promise, fulfillment and success could not prevent lynchings and nothing provided assurance. The televised variety and game shows, picturesque sprawling golfing greens, camper trailers, and 'rock and roll', the manufactured delights, the silent, sober, stable messages could Not ensure protection for Negroes and other minorities. By any measure life couldn't endorse racial equity. Quiet tears would fall in that cold atmosphere.

****

Anita and Carol Bernstein were in their early teens when the family turned away from the wandering life they'd been living, and settled down in a nice Philadelphia community. With that move the world took on a whole new brighter meaning.

Anita and sister Carol adapted well to the new status their parents put in place. Both girls totally embraced the normal, higher standard, socially and in every way. They attained college degrees, with Anita who attended University of Pennsylvania attend where she received a Masters' Degree in Social Work. Carol received a four-year-degree in music at the University of Pennsylvania to become a high school teacher in that field.

In other words, the big change that the Bernsteins' made afforded them a comfortable, higher, better way of living!

****

"You can't be serious, saying you want to marry Anita Bernstein, the daughter of former hippies is not our kind; she comes from the gutter, they're vagabonds. You both are too young any way to be thinking about marriage. The right girl will come along. But I know one thing, Anita Bernstein isn't that girl. We have a lot built up in you and your sister, Judy. Our whole family going back forever has expectations that we "Eddie, Anita comes from a family of Hippies. How can you even think about a girl from a background like that? You come from a longline of successful people. You're an attorney, and even served in the diplomatic corp. You don't get all of that with a weak background!

There's a very interesting story concerning Eddie Ramsey when he was quite young and was employed in a United States Diplomatic position. You'll hear about that later.

Eddie Ramsey was a young attorney when he and Anita Bernstein met. He'd just failed attempts at a diplomatic career. The elevated position took him a long way from jobs he had as a teen. This is particularly so with a job that he had back then.

Eddie Ramsey didn't have anything handed to him. Even before high school he held a variety of jobs. Among those earlier jobs, he'd delivered telephone directories to Philadelphia residents, and was bus boy at restaurants, Speaking of restaurants, he once encountered a ridiculous situation at a nightclub/restaurant that could've cost him his life.

"I need for you to go out there and do a act for me, kid. I been hearin' ya sing when Toni Diangelo's performin.' Kid, you sing good. Toni can't make it in t'night. So, get out there and sing whatever the audience ask." The big, burly gruff-sounding Italian restaurant manager told Eddie a song to do with the band." He'd worked all that summer as a bus-boy, and knew his boss wasn't playing. To his salvation, his voice cooperated somehow, and it was the same with his ability on stage. In a situation like this, Eddie pulled off his white apron, spruced up as much as possible, and stepped out on the big platform. He went over to the band's director, whispering the name of the song he'd been ordered to do.

"That ole black magic has me in a spell. That ole black magic that you weave so well….." He did a fair rendition of the song. Most importantly, he spotted him in the audience smiling and nodding yes, when he ended the song. When audience members shouted out songs for him to sing, he did them and everyone seemed pleased

****

Forty-year-old Salome Ughani realized the power she had over young diplomat Eddie Ramsey, just twenty-seven. Romance between them crystalized from the moment she walked into his office at the Embassy one day and they locked eyes. The older woman and much younger man became lost in a sea of love. There were times when she could not bring herself to that disposition, when she felt stripped of all reason because of her compelling love, a married woman for another man, and someone as young as one of her two sons. On this particular evening with the two of them in his nice, cozy apartment, she rose from the bed after they'd been wrapped in demanding, commanding love-making.

"Ed, I have to say this. We have to end this relationship." He looked perplexed.

"What brought this on? I love you, Salome, you know that. What did I do wrong? I thought you loved me, what are you saying?" he said, feeling confused, deeply hurt. "I can't recall any conflicts between us. What happened?" he seemed near tears. He never found a woman he'd felt as comfortable with as Salome Ughani. Not only did her astounding tall, smooth, slender looks draw him to her, her calm, compassionate personality drew him to her. Plus she believed in fighting injustice of any kind. Having grown up in a poor village near Addis Ababa in Ethiopia, witnessing hunger, and harshness of life for girls and women all around had made her sensitive to the misfortune of others. Her sisters and female cousins and the other girls she'd known had been forced into marriage by the time they were twelve or thirteen. Good fortune was on her side and made it possible for her to have schooling something that was not the case for most females. The English-operated school taught the students well. And then, she earned a scholarship to attend a secretarial college. That was how she'd landed the job at the Ethiopian Embassy, and at twenty became the wife of fifty-five-year-old high official Abdul Ughani.

"Eddie, we cannot continue this affair. It would be dangerous for you and me if my husband found out. We're taking too many chances. You must leave the embassy, return to America and form a new life for yourself. It's over for you and me."

A bomb explosion could not have hit him harder, turning away from his deep love for her, feeling no one could ever take her place. He'd just experienced the worst condemnation ever, and felt as though hopelessness and dejection had spread a tent over his life.

As much as he tried he felt he couldn't exist unless he made another attempt to reconnect with Salome. At the new job assignment at the State Department in Washington D.C., he requested, he couldn't focus. Nothing about his life made sense. *I have to see her, if only to hold her for a moment, feel her next to me, and maybe reawaken something.* Two months since the break-up he planned a trip to see her. The plan would remind her of the love they'd shared, and she'd want him back, willing to risk everything to establish that amazing romance they'd had once again. He'd do this in spite of her negative response when he'd called her often and spoken to her. 'I can't talk to you. It's over. We can't resume anything. Good-bye, Eddie.' Essentially, that's how she'd respond every time he called.

The flight to Addis Abba went without any problems, and he sat in a rented car on a street within eye sight of the estate where she lived. Since that morning he'd sat unseen in an area behind tall shrubbery that hid the car. Finally around 2pm he saw her tall, beautiful form leaving her home. His heart began to pound with anticipation and love. It became difficult not to jump out of the car and go after her, embrace her, remind her of everything they'd shared and lost. Nevertheless he sat there and watched her leave her beautiful manor, and back out of the garage. He eased his car away and slowly followed. *I'll go to where she goes and then make myself known.* He had to take precautions for both their sake. He worried what the consequences might be if anyone noticed them together, and it got back to her husband. Finally, after a very long drive, perhaps five miles, she turned down a tiny road. After driving for about a mile she pulled into a small restaurant parking area. She left the car and went inside at which time he instantly got out of his car and followed her. The moment he entered the tiny restaurant, his heart dropped. She leaned over and kissed a very young man sitting at a table. As a matter of fact, he thought the man looked younger than he. *This can't be*, he thought deeply disappointed.

"Salome, what are you doing?" he told her, crushed and sounding lost and deeply hurt when he managed to talk with her, quietly in the restaurant. "Who is that?"

"This is my lover. Sorry Eddie, but he is my lover now." She almost sounded matter-of-fact. I'm so sorry. I didn't expect you to come see me. I kept telling you it was over between us. But you didn't listen. I'm sorry."

"So, this is what you do. You're always looking for someone younger, and you think is better. I get it" he told so hurt he had to cool the fierce anger rising in him and with that, he turned and left the restaurant. That incident left a wound on his heart that would be difficult to heal, but he never tried to see her, or contact her after that.

Nonetheless, for the sake of her life, not his, he quit the Ethiopian Embassy and returned to Philadelphia, carrying her heart with him forever.

Chapter Three

"Yes, I'm responding to the ad for a live-in nanny. I'm Anita Bernstein", she nervously answered. When Anita Bernstein was twenty-four sought work to help pay for her Doctorate Sociology degree she was seeking. "I talked with you on the phone yesterday. The upper-class Watkins family lived in one of the city of Philadelphia's affluent sections.

"Come in, come in. We have three rambunctious boys, I'd better let you know that right away," Twenty-nine-year-old Marian Watkins was tall, statuesque very light skinned with straight, long, wavy brunette hair, and gorgeous.

"Your home is lovely," she remarked, looking around as Marian Watkins escorted her to the living room. Inside, the large Victorian house was beautifully decorated and was quite impressive.

"We've had that ad in the Philadelphia Inquirer for over a week. You're only the second person to show any interest. My husband and our three sons are in the den. Let me take you to meet them. I like your warm friendly smile," she said, leading her through the voluptuous surroundings. "I have a feeling you're just the person John and I are looking for."

Tall handsome John Watkins stood, and greeted her with a hand shake. The thirty-year-old attorney handled litigation for the NAACP. Marian Watkins taught elementary school in the Germantown school district in Philadelphia. John Jr., ten, Robert, seven and Charles, three, remained seated but looked at Anita with smiles.

She didn't have to do any household chores, a domestic came to the house once a week for that. Anita's job mainly involved providing good care, and attention to the couple's three boys.

"I love you, Anita," the youngest boy Charles said, reaching his arms around her. All three boys gave her much affection, and she returned their warm feelings. She immediately developed a fondness for the three handsome boys she found delightful to be around. She enjoyed taking them to on outings to hilly Fairmount Park, or the Philadelphia Zoo, or to the Ben Franklin and Art Museums, etc., but the saying 'boys will be boys' is so true). However, she formed a good relationship with the family; because of the Watkin's, she even got into the political side of life-joining demonstrations and protest marches around the city. She met Eddie Ramsey at a rally.

Anita became one of thousands joining a strong Civil Rights movement happening in the South with sit-ins and civil rights protests with boycotts at some establishments around the City of Philadelphia. She often showed up with the attorney and his wife at demonstrations involving a major effort underway to change the discrimination in practice at a prestigious all-White private school for boys in Philadelphia. The philanthropist who founded the school designated it for poor 'White' boys only). On this particular chilly evening Anita with a large crowd of demonstrators rallied outside the walls of the White-only private school when a placard caught her attention. "A school just ain't right that's all White." The sign's carrier was a good looking tall, ruddy-complexioned man. Eddie Ramsey smiled and winked at Anita, and called out, "Hey, good lookin!' And then going over to her, "I'm , and just who are you? MMMMMmmmm!" He had a lean, well-conditioned body that could be noticed through the heavy wool sweater and tailored dark slacks. He was hatless and his hair was short and wavy. Anita wore a thick long coat, a scarf around her neck and a red tam. Single Eddie Ramsey was one of the most noted attorneys in Philadelphia. With all of his good looks, he possessed a lot more going for him: charm, a caring, sensitive nature and more. Love was immediate for Anita Bernstein and Eddie Ramsey and in a very short time the handsome couple had become engaged.

****

Anita had been in her downtown Philadelphia apartment, on the living room sofa absorbed in a book when someone rang her doorbell.

"Hi, sweetheart, I told you I had an NAACP meeting, but I thought I'd like for you to come along, I wanted you with me. Get dressed, and let's go," Eddie Ramsey said, at the door. The large room at the NAACP headquarters seemed packed with everyone who belonged to the organization. As they entered, it surprised Anita to see so many present. Then, more shocking, a loud cheer went up, and immediately, he dropped down on his knees.

"I discovered that I'm so deeply in love with you. Please, say you'll be mine, forever. I've discovered we belong together, and I want you to be my wife. Just give me the chance and I'll show you how much I care. I'll love you forever and ever. I don't want life without you, I have to have you and love you. Will you marry me?"

"Yes, darling, yes," she told him with tears of joy running down her face.

Chapter Four

Delores Ramsey and son were together in the beautiful high-ceilinged parlor of the Ramsey family's extravagant home. He could not have been more resentful listening to his mother scorning Anita. However soft-spoken as Delores Ramsey was publicly, she could be ruthless in private. She was staunch about protecting the honorable image of the Ramsey's.

"They left that lifestyle a long time ago. Her father's a prominent physician, and Mrs. Bernstein a practicing social worker," he responded, frustrated and angry, wishing he could turn her vile reaction off like a spigot. Nonetheless he listened to the horrible things his mother said against Anita, the woman he so deeply loved. Anger began building up inside of him. "Mother, you can't be saying Anita's not good enough for families like the Ramsey's. If you are, that's just wrong," Ed Ramsey said in contempt over his mother's reactions to the girl he loved and admired. He could understand her feelings long ago, when she tried to dissuade him from hanging around with a girl he met while in college. "You need to stop spending time with that girl. I know you say it's just friendship, but that girl is out of the ghetto, and suppose people think she and you are involved. She and son were together in the beautiful high-ceilinged parlor of the Ramsey family's extravagant home. An amazing thing occurred in her life the moment Clara Waters and Eddie Ramsey became best friends, the teenager could envision life with even more optimism; some of the feelings of inadequacy she suffered seemed to melt away once she met the handsome, tall and young. Clara couldn't get over her unusual circumstance that someone from a family that yielded wholesomeness and sobriety would want to spend time with a person from a lowly background and in a horrific situation as she. She almost felt as though she'd discovered a haven in him. He was a fire escape from the sense of helplessness that sometimes made her feel trapped. He was a bridge to a better way of looking at life. She could dismiss a lot of the feelings of deep regret and embarrassment she had concerning the poverty lay all around her, the poor conditions she and her siblings and mother lived under. In every way Eddie Ramsey increased the value of her life. Even in the things he did that were small, he stretched her capacity to comprehend everything, and in the end, be absorbed by life in a way she would relish being a part of life. She was certain that the sense of affirmation she felt because of him would be missed; if she relied upon her personal viewpoint, something might not have been present which would make a very important connection possible for a brighter future. Not only was their relationship well-matched on academic and intellectual levels, both were under the realization that what they were doing together was of an enormous benefit. Clara would never forget the marvelous experience as his high school prom date. What an example of how much larger he made her perception of life.

Clara couldn't believe Eddie Ramsey had asked her to the high school prom, it was something she hadn't even thought about, and felt honored as she never had. And realizing he'd gone head to head with his mother, Delores just because he'd insisted on being her best friend, made him taking her to the prom even more special. The young couple joined with three other pairs for the exciting gala evening. They met up at the extraordinary, almost mansion like, home of one of the girls. Clara couldn't help being amazed, fascinated by the luxury surrounding her when she and Eddie drove up the long driveway and parked. Eddie's friend's prom date, a very fair-complexioned, beautiful girl opened the double doors to them. Inside, Clara found the home inside even more amazing than the outside. She thought she'd entered the home of a celebrity. The host ushered her and other two girls prom dates up the long spiraling staircase to her bed room that looked larger than the entire house she'd grown up in. The girls fussed over themselves, and returned down stairs so the four couples could be on their way to the greatly anticipated prom.

After he vacated her life, she felt almost nothing except rejection and dejection. Once she was returning a book to the library, it was the library located in his neighborhood where she and Eddie Ramsey had gone often. She went to this library for the closeness she experienced being in a place they'd been together. It was raining hard, and she began running to hasten to get inside out of the pouring rain. As fate would have it, the book, a very important biography she had read and enjoyed, fell to the wet ground and was pelted by rain. Before she could retrieve the book, the pages and jacket were wet through and through. The book appeared to be ruined. Tears of sadness fell down her cheeks. And, then, she looked up to see walking on the other side of the street, to avoid him seeing her with his new high school girlfriend. At this point, heartsick, she wanted to dissolve as the rain pounding the ground and disappearing, she felt so much hurt and much hopelessness.

****

Eddie Ramsey could not have been more resentful listening to his mother scorning Anita. However soft-spoken as Delores Ramsey was publicly, she could be ruthless in private. She was staunch about protecting the honorable image of the Ramsey's.

"My intention is to keep our family in an upright position. Stopping you from experiencing love and happiness is not my intention," she responded, tears falling down her face. However, in truth the situation had taken her back to disheartening times she experienced with his father. She wanted to prevent her son from following in his father's misguided footsteps. She worried the fruit had not fallen far from the tree, and he'd do some of the hurtful things his unfaithful father had. She withheld telling him that his father's seeds had been tossed all over the place. She knew of two children he'd fathered.

"Eddie, Anita comes from a family of Hippies. How can you even think about marrying a girl from a background like that?"

"I'm in love with Anita Bernstein, Mother. Did you hear that? Love, love, love her as I've never loved anyone. And I'll probably always love her. Now what? What do you have to say to that? And, guess what? I love her so much I'm going to marry her." There was something very powerful that Delores Ramsey had to bring to her mind about herself, she had not always been privileged.

Delores and her siblings had moved from a lowly social and financial position after their mother, Laura married Ralph Bayard, a successful businessman. That marriage to Ralph happened following the surprising death of her husband William who died of a heart attack at the early age of thirty-seven. Laura was left to raise four children ages thirteen, twelve, nine and seven. Delores was gifted with gorgeous looks and could easily attract another husband. Financially-set Ralph Bayard owned five successful restaurants in Philadelphia and in other northeast cities.

Nonetheless, Ralph Bayard governed Laura and her children and the household with a heavy hand. Laura could barely stand anything about her husband and his domineering, demeaning, harsh ways. With all of his money, he was a stickler about everything, keeping track of the smallest things. "Do you need another napkin? Use the one you have, napkins cost." He nastily demanded of Delores when she reached for a napkin at the kitchen table, because the one she'd been using was soiled. According to him everything in and outside of the household had a price tag, and he commanded how every single penny got spent. His controlling personality made him difficult to live with. It got to the point that at the dinner table seeing him eat made her cringe, but she managed to remain silent because he had certainly made life better according to the kind of home and the wealthy community where they now lived. Another matter made life with him difficult: "I'll see whoever I want. You don't decide who my friends. I'm, a businessman, and deal with all kinds of people, including lots of women." Thinking of her and her children, Laura maintained silent in every situation, thankful for the high station in life she and her children now had. No matter how dissatisfying his put downs and demands, he'd made a huge difference, pulled them up from the bottom of life. Delores and her siblings felt grateful as their mother for where Ralph Bayard had brought them.

Delores Ramsey easily adopted her mothers' silent, stoic attitude dealing with her own husband, Dr. Henry Ramsey. She accredited her stepfather for the life she had, for putting her in the situation to be able to meet Dr. Henry Ramsey. The two young people met at a private high school, and fell in love and eventually married and began a family.

As though he were thinking along the same lines, "Mother," he calmly began, "Have you ever known me to father any children?" He looked at his mother, his face deeply saddened. "I loved women, even some who did not love me, he said thinking back to Salome. "Can your elevated, sophisticated mind grasp the fact that I've tried to respect women, and myself? You can't cast off Anita. I refuse to let you demean her, and her family. Get ready, because you and Dad and everyone will accept Anita as my wife," he defiantly said, and walked out of the living room, leaving his mother, her mouth agape, startled.

There's something else about socialite, high standard Delores Ramsey. As staunch as she was about protecting the Ramsey's honorable image there was something that few knew about sophisticated Delores, secretly she was an alcoholic which she defended. "I suffer from narcolepsy," Delores told everyone due to her inability to stay awake. The truth, however rest on the fact that drinking too much made her want to sleep.

The poor section in Philadelphia where Delores Ramsey and her siblings spent their childhood, she had little to inspire and lift their spirits. Nonetheless, everyone in the community worked hard and cooperated, and overcame the hardships they faced. For Delores and her family hardship hit worse. Luther, her youngest died tragically at age five. The fateful day went like this.

The morning of the Fourth of July you felt the atmosphere dripping with heat and humidity and anticipation of a fun day at Philadelphia's Fairmount Park. Women prepared lots of food for a picnic at the luscious grounds where they'd spread a blanket and enjoy activities and Independence Day program with a crowd packing the City Park. Delores and her brothers and sisters immediately took to the wonderful grounds, playing softball, and running about. Five-year-old Luther had wandered off from the family and the other children playing. He climbed one of the tallest hills and had started down when the youngster lost his footing, tumbling to the street below into the path of an on-coming semi. Young Luther died instant. Luther's tragic accident sent some family into shock and pain.

Delores could never put her young brother's death out of her mind, and after, would no longer play on the hilly vacant lot all the children called Indian Hill.

Despite growing up in an adverse environment in Philadelphia, her childhood presented her with extraordinary, inspiring things. The neighborhood transferred a feeling of hope and promise. It could even show her a stairway to heaven. In that regard an atmosphere of music bound Delores Robinson Ramsey; its magical components escalated her life. Examples of exhilarating music included certain uplifting songs included "Brazil." Music played such a powerful role in her life as a young person, that she lived through love ballads; and thirsted on the illusion of incredible love and romance. All of her dreams for love and happiness had been planted back then-the man she would marry, the children they would have together. Throughout her youth, romantic songs shared a future of immense hope and love; they transported her from the unrewarding, bad effects in the surroundings trampling on her, cancelling her dreams. The Broadway show tunes she listened to had magnificent appeal as a place lost in time, lulling and magical. One of the ways in which she achieved this was by being studious. She passed up no opportunity to learn something which served to help her grow. A neighbor woman helped enormously in that way. Perhaps in her middle years, Sandra Anderson, soft-spoken and reasonably cultured was the parent of a childhood friend. She helped promote her sense of the world. Mrs. Anderson worked for the government in a clerical capacity. Essentially she was at the end of a family of high status-the family's elevation had been erased or nullified. Nevertheless she held on to the high respect and those things in her background that benefited her. She took a certain extra measure of pride in her children, her husband and the operation of her household. (One was the fact that she'd attended "Girls' High School." The high-ranking school was reserved for the most scholastic, high-achieving girls in the Philadelphia area. Among other things from her solid, upstanding background she received extensive musical training as a girl).

From a young girl Delores Robinson Ramsey felt a sense of goodness springing up around her as she chased after a rainbow and dreamed of an island of love. She and her siblings enjoyed the Saturday matinee, books-mostly books they borrowed from the local library and there were church and school activities. They and other children also played in Fairmount Park. And although her environment was lacking, she was determined to improve her life. She would cross the Schuylkill River Bridge to the park grounds of the Philadelphia Museum of Art. The experiences she had there and in other places would lift and transport her.

Chapter Five

Delores Ramsey easily adopted her mothers' silent, stoic attitude dealing with her own husband, Dr. Henry Ramsey. (She blamed Ralph Bayard, her step-father with his disregard and unfair treatment for why she expected so little in regard to respect from her husband, Dr. Henry Ramsey) Delores and Dr. Henry Ramsey met at a private high school, and fell in love and eventually, five years later married and began a family.

As though he were thinking along the same lines, "Mother," he calmly began, "Have you ever known me to father any children?" He looked at his mother, his face deeply saddened. "I loved women, even some who did not love me, he said thinking back to Salome. "Can your elevated, sophisticated mind grasp the fact that I've tried to respect women, and myself? You can't cast off Anita. I refuse to let you demean her, and her family. Get ready, because you and Dad and everyone will accept Anita as my wife," he defiantly said, and walked out of the living room, leaving his mother, her mouth agape, startled.

The wedding of Anita Bernstein and Edward Ramsey was astounding! Everything from when the couple took their vows at the Ramsey's St Luke Episcopal Church in Philadelphia, to the splendid display of music, menu and decoration at the reception, everything that day could be labeled sensational, as you would expect with Delores Ramsey in charge!

The wedding that joined Anita and Eddie beautifully portrayed a couple synchronized in devotion and love. Dressed in white, she was as beautiful as an angel. Handsomely attired in tuxedo, he could not keep his eyes off of her because of how elegant and lovely she looked. She beamed with admiration for the man accepting her commitment. His parent's and others in his family, Julia and Joshua Bernstein and the

Brown's and all of the relatives of both families and friends of the families exuded the utmost happiness into the atmosphere. They were effusive with smiles-even if for some it was forced or faked. There were seven bridesmaids and groomsmen. Elva, her sister Carol's friend from her California days had come for the wedding. The joyous wedding was brought to a level of incredible joyousness and fun because of Elva's lively contribution during the reception at the Sheraton Hotel in Philadelphia. She threw the ballroom into delirious laughter when she came sliding down the banister of the long hotel staircase.

Eddie Ramsey's best friend throughout their school years, Clara Waters was an invited guest at the wedding of Eddie Ramsey and Anita Bernstein. The entire time Clara endured a heavy, sorrowful spirit witnessing the love of her life giving his heart in wedding vows to Anita, instead of her. She'd never moved in any way from her original love for him; for that matter no one had come into her life who could replace Eddie Ramsey. It was her hope that if she'd kept her heart open he'd returned to her to be his lifetime partner. Over all of the years since their youth until now, her deep love for Eddie Ramsey had not diminished. At the reception Eddie came over to her at the table where she was. In response she stood up from the table. "Clara, I'll always be grateful to you for the balance you put into my life. You are the most, genuine, natural, and caring friend I've ever had," Eddie told her earnestly. He then pulled her to him hugging her with great affection. Tears fell down her cheeks, as an unexplainable mixture of feelings captured Clara.

Soon after they'd married, Eddie Ramsey Jr. was born, and less than two years later, Paul George Ramsey followed.

Chapter Six

Twenty-six-year-old Carol Bernstein found life totally boring, and that included her job as a High School music teacher something she'd done since graduating college. She began to strongly consider re-locating. California began calling her; its broad, inviting landscape seemed to be waiting for her arrival. She'd applied for a government job on an Army Base, and got hired since the Viet Nam War had required personnel at military bases. And the ones in California became especially important since those military installations interacted with the casualties of war in a large way.

Carol Bernstein thought she could locate little of an enlivening nature. Sadly she arrived to discover Los Angeles, California a featureless site when compared to other places everywhere she'd been.

With all of the imagination she'd drawn of Los Angeles, California, the picture of that city conjured up as one of little fascination, and that included South Central L.A. She came to see South Central similarly as a spiritless, uninventive, inert location. This section of Los Angeles is stilted, and not a 'happening place.' And for that matter she realized that the case with Los Angeles in general. She experienced it as a place without a genuine spirit of regeneration. She witnessed the hippie aspect even more expanded than the one she'd grown up in; lost to life in doorways, or begging in front of stores, seeming as lechers, drop-outs of society. (In a natural context for the city as a whole, the landscape, she saw it suffering from a lack of greenery and because of it, not in the least invigorating).

Even against the frivolity of Hollywood reigning in its midst, Los Angeles possessed few affirming qualities and features. Expressing her true sense about Los Angeles, California, she said about it: "the horrific solidifying effect of '1960s' War in Viet Nam, and lost souls that came out of the 'Sixties'-something she wished she had not experienced-something uninspiring looms in the environment, "There's almost nothing that makes me want to stay in this place."

Carol transferred her life to a town near San Francisco, and working at a Government job she'd applied for at a U.S. Army Post outside of Hartly, the small town where she was renting a small house. (Except for the Army Post, Hartly was basically colorless and dull. Nonetheless, the town was within driving distance to San Francisco and Sacramento, and near livelier places to go).

Carol Bernstein found working in the mailroom at the U.S. Army hospital rewarding. Even though she wasn't medically administering to the young soldiers who'd been wounded in the Viet Nam war, she had the sense that she was doing something encouraging. Encouraging also, at her mailroom job Carol met Elva Davis, a GI's wife and her seven-year-old son, Benjamin. Elva Davis who had come from Philadelphia became Carol's very special friend.

"Can me and Boo move in with you while Jack's doing a one-year tour in Iraq"? Elva Davis smiling asked, assured of a positive response from her Bestie Carol Bernstein.

"Girl, you didn't even have to ask. I'd be glad to have you and Boo here. You'll be good company," Carol told her smiling. She welcomed the prospect of having her friend and seven-year-old son come stay with her. In a real sense, she sometimes felt a little bit lonely with just her and young son Benjamin, who she called Boo, living alone.

She appreciated Jack Davis for marrying her, and raising her young child, Boo as his own. They lived as a military family in a bungalow near the Army base. After three short years together Elva found herself in an unhappy marriage. It was clear to her that trouble faced their relationship.

"Jack, please don't go to the NCO Club. Stay home, with me, please. I don't feel safe when you're out of the house. And, I worry about you. You're out there drinking and driving. Anything could happen."

"Girl, where did you put my car keys…? Sergeant Jack Davis angrily asked, lifting the pillows on the couch; angry and cursing, he wildly went throughout the house looking every place thinking she might have placed his keys somewhere he couldn't locate. She looked on helplessly, sobbing and begging him not to go out, drinking and driving, to no avail. 'Listen, where I come from a man don't let no woman tell him what to do. My daddy wouldn't think of etting' my mama tell him when and where he could...go.' And then he might go into a song, a Blues singer made popular which he felt described his life, and drunkenly begin to sing: "I don't want no woman tellin' what to do. I don't want n woman, tellin' me what to do. Woooo…woooo….oooo….ooooo," his head thrown back, howling, he was doing an imitation of a wolf…his 'call of the wild.' (Once, trying to prevent him from driving while drunk Elva had grabbed young Boo, and run out to the car and taken off. From the rear view mirror she saw him standing outside the house, waving his arms wildly, shouting horrible names at her as she tore down the street).

Sergeant Jack Davis couldn't resist Cam Thi Nguyen, a beautiful Vietnamese girl he met one evening. The twenty-three-year-old caught his attention the moment he stepped in the NCO Club and eyes found her tending bar. Much taller than you'd expect for an Asian woman, she had flowing dark brown hair and staggering brown eyes. Immediately attracted, he straight away headed for the bar, leaving his three G.I. companions laughing at their compelled buddy as they went toward a table of some pretty smiling girls flirting with them. The NCO Club was a barrack-style building on the Army base in Phan Rang, Viet Nam with a lovely garden and patio where most couples wandered outside.

"How about a bourbon and soda," he told her, smiling broadly at the bar. She smiled, nodding yes, and instantly turned to fix what he ordered.

"Hi, I'd like to introduce myself, he said right away. And, your name is?" She told him her as she mixed his drink and handed it to him. Her beauty was compelling, and he also couldn't help noticing gracefully she moved, almost a dancer's litheness.

"I'm Army Sergeant Jack Davis. I admired instantly. I hope you don't misread my advances. I'm for real. I'd like to get to know you if you don't belong to anybody."

"My name Cam Thi Nguyen. I no belong to anyone. I work here for about six months. I don't see as I remembah seein' you here," she said with a broad smile, realizing the Army Sergeant's handsomeness. His heart beat so hard he hoped the pounding didn't show through his brown dress uniform shirt.

"I arrived here a week ago, here for a year's tour. I hope I don't sound pushy, but I'd like to see you. Are you available? What I mean is. I've seen the garden. It's a beautiful place out there. Would you care to go there when you get a break?" She seemed happy for the invitation, and told yes. Later, when she had a break, the two went outside into the darkness holding hands. They walked around the beautiful gardens under a crescent moon and a violet sky until the club shut down for the night.

I don't have to tell that the two found themselves caught up in love. The couple would meet whenever he could get away and spent rapturous times together. Months went by swiftly, and he was called in and his year was over in Viet Nam.

"I don't want to leave you, Cam Thi. I want to spend the rest of life with you. It can happen if you'd become my wife, and come and live in the U.S. You know it'll take time to get a divorce from my wife. But I'll do that, and whatever it takes so that we can be together."

"I'm expecting our child", Cam Thi calmly told him.

"Where is my damn keys?" Jack Davis asked his wife, Elva in a threatening voice. To her regret, he located the keys she'd hidden to prevent him getting in the car and taking off drunk. Forlorn and crying, she watched from the window as he drove away. That night he lost his life in a horrendous car accident-he hit a power pole that crash in on him. Regrettably, Elva Davis had a drinking problem herself!   Elva Davis entered the mailroom looking very upset. "Girl, I'm mad as hell. I just come from the dental clinic. I had a appointment ta get my teeth cleaned and a check-up. 'N' the dentist refused ta do anything on me. Come talkin' 'bout I had been drinkin.' Hell, I wasn't drunk! Hell, I'd just had a coupla 'hits,' he oughta be glad I didn't have a later appointment, or I'da came there 'tanked.' You know me. There was no end to the number of incredible, funny episodes circumscribing the life of Elva Davis. Not only did Elva amuse her, but Carol had to admire her friend for the self-motivation and the kind of bravery she demonstrated. The best friend also impressed her with her approach to staying in tip-top shape: Elva maintained a health a diet and a rigorous exercise regime.

Elva Brown, at just sixteen struck out on her own, with her one-year-old son Benjamin, (Boo). Aspiring to make her life better, getting away from a miserable home life, she left Philadelphia for California. It had been a miracle that someone so young could transplant the way she had successfully done. She tried from a young girl trying figure a way to take herself out of the horrendous household. Once, a relative's visit introduced the idea to consider joining the military once she reached the eligible age.

"This is Mimi, Fugi and Miko," the Japanese US Army Sergeant with a gleaming friendly face told them. He and his wife and three young daughters accompanied Sergeant Janet Brown, a WAC, in uniform and sharp-looking. Harriet Brown's cousin had come to stop by with her companions because a change assignment had the group to Fort Dix Army Post in nearby New Jersey. Elva and her siblings couldn't stop staring with envy at the Japanese family in their midst. Her mother's cousin Sergeant Janet Brown attracted Elva most of all. She'd never seen a uniformed Negro female in person. *I want to be a WAC when*

I'm old enough, she thought wistfully. She kept thinking about the evening and the impression it had. Nonetheless, the sight of her uniformed cousin had the greatest effect for it caused her to have a positive future she envisioned becoming a WAC like her cousin Sergeant Janet Brown.

"I was fifteen-years-old when I had Boo. I became pregnant as result of rape. They never found the man who showed up in the bedroom I shared with two younger sisters one night, and gagged and raped me. From childhood on, I felt like damaged goods. I grew up in a poor-behind family, one of seven children." Elva Davis had shared some of her past with Carol, her best friend.

Elva and her three sisters and three brothers suffered the worst kind of abuse and neglect. The siblings endured a wretched situation that included having to cope with the mother Harriet's boyfriends who were in good supply in and out of the household. Elva tried to protect her siblings from the sexual predators hanging around. Then the mother's boyfriend arrived, a man named Gilbert who posed the worst kind of threat. Young Elva could expect Gilbert to take advantage of her when her mother zonked out, in an alcoholic stupor, which happened often. He sexually abused her from age ten until she left home at age sixteen. Because of her mother's alcohol addiction, Elva had to do for the younger ones-fixing a bowl of cereal, or giving the baby a bottle, changing diapers, dressing all of them, and doing almost everything that children need to survive. Sadly there wasn't any relative in the area to turn to since her mother had moved to Philadelphia from down south. Alcohol and Gilbert's constant physical abuse had complete control over Elva's mother Harriet. The siblings would hide under a bed to shield themselves from those frightening times that he badly beat their mother. Reporting anything was not going to help. The boyfriend Gilbert held young Elva hostage, her head swam with his threats to her and everyone in the house if she opened her mouth about any of the horrible things that he did. "I got somebody ta baby sit Boo, let's go somewhere ta'night. I called Donald 'n' William," Elva said at her typewriter, working on some records in the US Army hospital mailroom where she and Carol Bernstein worked.

"Where we going"? Carol asked, also busy at her desk.

"Where do we always go"?

Buck Sergeant William Truitt and Corporal Donald Lawson along with Elva and Carol had formed a bond. It was the custom of the group of four to go to the NCO Club every Friday and Saturday night. Soldiers, many waiting to be shipped to Viet Nam packed the NCO Club.

Carol once had a conversation with a soldier, around twenty that touched her heart.

"I leave tomorrow for Phan Rang. The young soldier from Panama told Carol, his eyes weakened by the many beers he'd consumed, and fear of the war prospects. She attempted to relieve some of the young soldiers' anxiety by speaking in Spanish she recalled from high school. That same evening Elva told her that their friends, Corporal Donald Lawson and Sergeant William Truitt had orders and would be leaving in about a week for Iraq. The two young soldiers did not return alive. For Carol and everyone, the worst part while working at the military hospital occurred with the constant arrival of bags with the bodies of young men killed in the jungles of Viet Nam.

Miss, can you give me my mail," a very young, black man in hospital garb said. That's alright. I'll come in there after it. You are so nice. And you're pretty. What's your name?" She instantly could see that the young man suffered with mental issues, and probably a shell shock victim. Her heart went out to the soldier who seemed so very young. However, she changed to become frightened when smiling broadly he began climbing over the counter of the mailroom office. She yelled out for help. Hospital staff immediately arrived and corpsmen took him back to his where he'd been confined.

To the great dismay of Elva Davis, she received a call with the tragic news that her twenty-one-year-old sister, Charlotte had been murdered. Her body was found behind the nightclub where she'd been working. The night before, someone had raped and strangled her to death. To this day the person responsible has not been found. Charlotte had always sought her own way. She never abided by a set of rules. Perhaps her untamed family situation had produced her reckless personality, in any case, she came to care little concerning how she lived her life, and tossed her cares to the wind. She did as she pleased. And like Elva, she'd left home as a teen fed up with her miserable living situation. She'd been deceitful and devious from a young girl. And as an adolescent she would sneak boys into her bedroom while everyone in the house slept. Her illicit sexual activity got her and a boy discovered in the basement. She only got worse, doing all kind unsavory, illicit things…prostitution is suspected as the cause for her death-a trick killed her. Nonetheless, Elva's recalled hearing about after she moved away concerning her sister and a relationship with an older man in the community. She suspected her sister went often to the neighbor's house for money in exchange for favors. Elva wondered could that man out of jealousy have involved killed her sister. She never brought it up just in case he'd had nothing to do with her sister's death.

Elva's youngest brother as well had come to a tragic end as his sister Charlotte. Rodney's homosexuality wasn't something he wanted to share with his sisters, or the rest of the family, or with anyone in the community. However, they suspected that he might tend that way by his actions and things he seemed interested in. One dark night, Rodney took his life, shooting himself in the head.

Chapter Seven

"Carol, you don't have to do this for me. I'm fine. You're doing just fine out there in California, why would you uproot yourself and come back this way?" In truth, the news that her daughter would come back east made Julia Bernstein glad for she missed her daughter terribly. And, her daughter felt no less the emptiness living so far away from her mother.

Twenty-three-year-old Carol Bernstein had experienced a dark passage that included the horror and ravages of the Viet Nam War, living in California. She'd felt dislocated the whole time she'd lived there. She found the California scene a continuation of the communal life she'd spent her early childhood. It seemed a place separated from a formulae for normal living, even formless a place open to its own appraisal, anybody's affectations, unapproved. It even appeared more unregulated than the commune she'd lived in as a young child. At least the group didn't reflect a large measure of the population as California seemed to. She would see hippie types everywhere, intermixing with the population, high, hanging out in doorways, and begging for money even as the Salvation Army might, in front of grocery stores and other kinds of markets high, and begging for money. Her childhood group never did that. However, it happened that the 'natural' landscape where she lived didn't present any appeal, it lacked prolific vegetation-woods, trees, that dominated the east coast and she'd grown used to.

From her first day arriving in the California area, Carol found the surroundings disappointing. Everything she saw seemed to present a reflection of what Carol and her sister Anita, and family and the group they lived with experienced- hellishness and disrepute, and social unrest).

"Oh, come on. You need to get out, see people. Meet some guys. Work isn't everything," co-worker Mary Jones, around Carol's age, in her middle twenties said, trying to convince her to come along to the USO. The two women worked for the U.S. Government building in downtown Philadelphia. Carol had been back in the city for six months, and hadn't gone anywhere except to her job. (It had been a hard decision, leaving behind Elva Davis and her child, Boo. But to continue living in Hartly, California, a place so opposite of what she wanted for herself was not something she could do. She decided it best to return to Philadelphia. Nonetheless, she didn't care to resume teaching school as a music teacher.)

"Oh, okay. But I don't want to," Carol responded reluctantly. She just couldn't get her spirits to rise. She'd had scarcely even spoken to a man. A guy or two had shown interest. Life just seemed flat and interesting. Nevertheless, she decided that going to the USO might uplift some young soldiers, and that was definitely not a bad thing, even if doing so didn't do anything for her doldrums.

The summer evening was warm and balmy as the two young women boarded the city bus, and rode across town to the USO. For some reason Carol felt that the evening was braced by magic, and hailed something romantic, a feeling of expectancy filled her heart. The two young women went inside a rather large, aging brick building and into a huge room where there were about fifty young G.I.s and women, however not nearly as many women. A long table had punch and lots of other refreshments, and there was an amateurish band was playing popular music. Some were dancing; while other couples were engaged in conversation; some of the G.I.s formed pockets. Carol spotted a tall, lanky, very handsome G.I. who was standing around having conversation with a couple of other young G.I.'s, and was instantly struck by romance. His eye caught hers, and he smiled sensuously and winked. Her smile in response was shy. He then began to stroll confidently over to where Carol and her friend were. Her heart really pounded when she saw him approaching her and her friend's table. She hoped she'd be the one he showed interest. He immediately asked her to dance, and she accepted.

She was floating on a cloud as she danced with the young, handsome soldier who told her his name was Jonathan Goodson.

That evening linked Carol Bernstein and Jonathan Goodson. It was a fast and furious courtship. She called her mother Julia the very night after her first date with Jonathan Goodson. The first thing she did was to jump on the telephone to call the one person she loved the most, and had always trusted with her life.

"Mama, I just met the man I'm going to marry. He's in the Service, his name is Jonathan Goodson." Julia had never heard her daughter express such happiness about anyone. To see her so excited, Julia instantly began thinking a wedding would take place, and not very long from then. She could see her beloved daughter on a journey to happiness, and felt it wouldn't be long before she became Mrs. Jonathan Goodson.

The marriage ceremony was an outdoor event that took place in rural Arkansas at the Goodson's family farm.

Jonathan Goodson came from a large rural family. His father, James Goodson owned a 300-acre cotton farm in the Arkansas Delta. Carol admired the lifestyle of his farm family. Albeit, the adult children in his family complained that life growing up had been so hard, but from all of her observations, life had been good for the Goodson's. (Although he was not exactly a prosperous the tall, robust father owner of a 300-acre cotton farm provided well for his family).

Jonathan's mother Lila, Little Flower was a full-bred native of the Matikoti tribe, the daughter of Giant Acorn, Chief of the Matikoti Indian tribe of around four hundred.

"I would like to welcome everyone to another Matikoti event," Giant Acorn announced standing in the center of the burgeoning crowd, a tall, big, strong man, looking proud and larger than life. 'Yeah, Yeah, Giant Acorn, 'the large assembled group of people cheered. "Before we get started, I'd like to make an important announcement." The impressive

Indian Chief, Jonathan's Grandfather stretched out an arm to Jonathan and Carol in the crowd. Five months pregnant Carol was next to Jonathan, sitting in chairs next to each other. "Big Acorn, Jonathan stand up." As Jonathan rose from his seat he threw a glance of happiness and pride to Carol. "Folks, Jonathan is the son of my daughter, Lila, to our tribe, Little Flower. I am proud to announce that soon he will make me a great grandfather again. (Pride filled Giant Acorn as well because he saw his tall, handsome grandson remaining faithful to his culture, standing strong as a Matikoti). As a matter of fact, Jonathan put to use many the skills taught him by the men of his mother's reservation. He demonstrated great ability working with his hands. He was especially good constructing boats that he carved or hewed out of wood. His woodworking talent led to a sideline job customizing boats.

"Jonathan, I think I'd like to give it a try." Carol was saying this as she gave her hand to Little Bull, one of Matt's young brothers-stunningly costumed-who'd come for her to join in the Matikoti dance. Jonathan was smiling as he replied, 'me, too', leaving the crowd of people they'd been standing among, so the three could enter the circle of dancers that was growing as others also were coming forward.

Jonathan and Carol Goodson went often to the reservation in the southern region of the state to visit his people. Carol never tired of being at the Matikoti Indian reservation. With every visit, the young married couple was given a huge welcome. What she especially enjoyed were the tribal dances the Matikoti's performed. They participated in the ritual dancing, or watched the dancers in their colorful, elaborate, primitive costume. The tribal dances went past fascination, and she was sometimes transformed, as she watched. One very primitive dance about a return to 'the land of memory' was so poignant it caused Carol to feel as though a movie about ancient warring tribes was being screened. (Darkness and peril were wild and furious. The sky was charcoal and tumultuous with Indian warriors riding giant horses, attacking other tribes with spears and arrows).

"Jonathan, I think I'm about to have the baby…it's too soon," Carol, worried and crying, she told her husband in the middle of the night. The baby didn't survive. Sadly, a year later when she became pregnant, that child didn't survive either when it was born prematurely.

The gypsy took her right hand, and held it, her dark eyes seeming to Carol to pierce her palm.

"What do you see? Is something wrong?" Carol asked, so nervous she began trembling, and regretting she'd come there. "I need to know why I lost my two babies, and what is in the future for me. What will happen if I become pregnant again?"

The psychic kept her deep gaze on the cards before her on the table. Carol began trembling in fear of what the psychic might report. "Yes. There is something." She looked up from the cards spread before her with a troubled faced. "A man, very handsome and upstanding is dressed in all black. That is all I can tell you." The woman turned her black pencil-lined eyes away and downward, as if she wanted to avoid having to report something terrible.

"There's more, isn't there? I'd like to know what it is", Carol nervously asked. She could tell the woman had more to say, "Please, tell me. I want to know."

With sad overtones the psychic softly spoke. "I see a man walking away from you. Your marriage appears to be in deep, deep trouble." There was a pause, and then she said in a voice that dropped to deeper depths, "I see another woman, he's going toward another woman." Hearing that Carol's face registered shock and fear, but she said nothing as she rose from her chair. The psychic said nothing further quiet and did not change her expression. She reached into her purse, handed the psychic twenty dollars. As she left the building she felt as if her legs would not carry her, however she did manage to get to her car. Once inside, her head fell against the steering wheel, and for a couple of minutes she sobbed uncontrollably in the car. As she was driving from the psychic's tiny parking lot, she asked herself, "Why? Why? Why did I go there?"

"Some angry White men showed up at the house for my younger brother, Elijah was sixteen, Morgan Goodson told someone, relating a tragic account in his background, talking about his father in particular and what he'd shared with him. "Then, my father was a sharecropper, and a good decent man. He and my mother brought up us thirteen children.' I'll never forgit that horrible day. My brother was working at a general store in town. And, it seems the White owner told the sheriff that he'd watched him for some time, and was sure that my brother was stealing from him. My mother says no one knew for sure if that was the truth. But you know how it was in those times it didn't matter, they didn't go by no law when it come to us. They took matters in their own hands. That evening, three trucks with White men pulled up at the house for my uncle. "Tell that boy ta bring his black behind out here. We got some unsettled bus'niss!" the leader of the ten men demanded. "He ain't here," father quietly told them, but they pushed him aside and came in, looking for my brother. As it was, he was hiding in the woods that surrounded the farm. And that's where they went searching and found him. They hanged him in those woods. That was the worst day of our lives!We buried Elijah, and right after the funeral neighbors helped pack us up, and we left that part of Arkansas, for a safer place in Arkansas where daddy bought the farm we have."

"Mama never had to work in the fields. Daddy thought she was too pretty, with her green eyes, and alabaster skin, and silky hair," voiced one of Jonathan's sisters. Carol found herself thinking that no matter what Jonathan's family experienced they could not have been nicer. She never felt that she and sister Anita and her mother Julia and father Joshua Bernstein comprised less of a family, even though a Hippie household. However, she had to admit Jonathan's family as an ideal family had more appeal. She was only two when the automobile accident took the life of her father. Even with Julia her mother, doing the best she could to stay in contact, sadly Carol's relationship to her mother's family in South Carolina, didn't compare with Jonathan's. Even though she and Anita visited her mother's family down south, she knew them only from a distance, and could only gleaned happiness from small instances. Wanting a closer connection with that way of life down south, everything, even the smallest thing they did for her, had the effect of something monumental. She relished even the simplest object or expression given, reading into it something deep and meaningful. Glee filled her over anything she'd receive from her mother's side of the family. Growing up, from her excitement, you'd have thought it came in a transatlantic bottle someone found, and handed over to her. She became excited whenever her grandmother in South Carolina sent an odd package or a cardboard box she'd filled with homegrown peanuts or pecans.

Regardless of the seasons and shortcomings, life seemed to settle very comfortably around Carol when she got to meet Jonathan's Arkansas family.

Interestingly, after Jonathan Goodson and Carol Bernstein married they looked to find a spot that replicated their backgrounds when deciding where to settle down. They went looking around and landed on a nice piece of property in a farming community in upstate Pennsylvania. (It almost seemed the decision to become farmers had a link to Jonathan and Carol's background-her mother Julia's South Carolina farming family, and the Arkansas family farm of his father)

Dr. Joshua Bernstein became the victim of a pancreatic cancer. Julia, Carol, Anita and Joshua Bernstein's family painfully witnessed his suffering and rapid decline. In less than two months the horrible ordeal had taken him to final rest.

A Jewish funeral took place at Beth Shalom, the synagogue in which Joshua Bernstein had grown up. A large gathering celebrated his home-going. Sniffles came from the pews where Julia, Anita, Carol, his parents, and family grieved. Others present included friends from the old days in the commune showing Joshua Bernstein their respect.

"Carol, I'm sorry about your Dad…such a good man, a real loss", Bernard Willis sadly said to Carol. I've always admired your Dad. "Thank you, Bernard. I appreciate you and the others thinking enough of my dad to come," she told him, wiping her eyes.

"It's been quite a long time, for sure. I, I. He stopped there. He had much more to tell her, but thought it best to keep everything shut up inside, as he'd done for at least ten years.

Bernard Willis had been admired throughout his life. Generally speaking, he was stellar in many aspects: in academics his grades in ever subject throughout school were the highest in his class- as well as other areas he excelled. He also excelled in football and in basketball, and was the president of the student council in high school and he spoke convincingly and with extraordinary skill. Tall, handsomeness didn't erase his shyness around girls, especially when it came to his feelings for Carol Bernstein. Carol Bernstein and Bernard Willis had been friends since Middle School when her parents and sister left the commune and assumed a normal life as a family. As excellent students and high achievers Carol would have to say that many opportunities came about due to her friend Bernard Willis: he encouraged her to join the Debate team, the World Affairs Council Club, plus other school activities, and even learned the game of Chess. Without a doubt she had his heart, but he could never get up the courage to let her know. *If only I could muster the courage to say you are the prettiest, most desirable girl at Dickerson High. I just wish I could tell you that; let you know how much you mean to me.* He would write Carol Bernstein letters, and then crumble them up, and toss them in the wastebasket. Without Carol knowing, his eyes almost never moved from where she sat in their high school English class. In her presence, always courage left him. If they had a conversation, he used humor to hide his shyness and how nervous he was. She was living inside of him as his secret love.

And then one day the worst kind of news came to him, "Hey, Bernard, did you hear the latest, Carol Bernstein got married?" an old buddy informed him. He felt a ton of bricks falling, crushing the love in his heart for her.

Bernard Willis completed seminary studies at a college in Massachusetts. Afterward he served as a staff minister at St. John United Methodist, his home church in Philadelphia. Bernard Willis would eventually become the church's operational minister.

It was no easy decision for Bernard Willis to give up his secret love, Carol Bernstein. "Hello there, Mrs. Bernstein. How's Carol? Have she and husband increased yet?' He hoped with all of his heart, the married couple had remained childless.

"We're always running into each other at these conferences and conventions. Why don't we have a cup of coffee and tea and get better acquainted," attractive, twenty-three-year-old Elaine Cartwright warmly suggested. Elaine Cartwright's father, Reverend Willard Cartwright presided over St Matthews United Methodist Church in Philadelphia. (The church had an enormous membership, and viewed as an architectural wonder). Single, tall lovely Elaine Cartwright, a third grade schoolteacher lived with her parents in their comfortable Philadelphia home. Bernard Willis was drawn to her startling beauty and appeal every time he saw her. He found himself looking forward to the meetings to spot her there, and smile or say hello. It wasn't just her startling beauty. Not only was Elaine Cartwright perfect in looks, her personality was without flaw he'd never met anyone as congenial and caring. (She was in that category with Carol Bernstein, his grandmother, Eunice, his Aunts Evelyn and Laura, plus his mother, Louise).

"I'll take you up on that offer. How about today, during the conference break?" That day started a marvelous courtship that would end in matrimony. An incredible wedding occurred, and two years later Bernard and Elaine Cartwright were blessed with their first child, a son, and blessed again when a girl came into the couple's lives two years later. Truly he enjoyed a high position in the church, a wonderful family, and his many other accomplishments. However with the good and solid life he'd attained, Bernard Willis could not erase Carol Bernstein from his thoughts.

Chapter Eight

Julia Bernstein's daughters, Anita and Carol and her husband's family thought that a trip to England would serve as a reprieve from the sorrow she lived with daily after her husband Joshua died. She'd suffered night and day after losing the only man she'd ever loved.

For the days she'd been in England, Julia had been restored by the sights and scenes. The verdant woodlands and countryside were impressive and uplifting. And the churches and castle ruins were interesting. Strangely, in both settings there seemed to be something lurking in the background such as elves, gnomes and fairies and other foreign creatures. The forest dwellers, which included Robin Hood and friends, from tales and middle-earth had come to life, although not really visible. Julia found the Westminster Abbey experience even more riveting. There in the archaic Gothic London building, her thoughts were stolen by the crypts-some of which were entombed in marble floors: Shakespeare, Sir Francis Drake, Sir Walter Raleigh, Henry the VII, Elizabeth and there were many other presences representative of England's antiquity.

The vacation renewed her to some degree. Upon returning to the states, she left the home she and her husband had shared, and moved in with Carol and Johnathan Goodson on their farm.

Chapter Nine

Carol and Jonathan enjoyed farm life and could not have experienced more love and happiness.

Carol thought she had a good neighbor and friend when she met Susanne Inverson. But she would discover heartbreak as a result of her neighbor.

Looking out into darkness, Carol saw the dark solemn image of an Amish family in a black horse and buggy galloping by on the highway across from the farm. It was a chilly autumn afternoon as she from a window in the warm, cozy kitchen. Her husband Jonathan was out in the field, atop his Bushhog harvesting corn. As she watched her husband at work in surroundings he loved, it produced in her feelings of deep, crushing love for him. A full moon spilled its bright light across the dark shadow that consumed the farm and terrestrial background: the shadow of night was spread across the fields of corn, barley and wheat, the trees, sheds and other outbuildings. She felt aware of the peaceful, magical presence of the universal in the submerged surroundings and was forced to say out loud: "God's universe is a place of peace, beauty and love." In the midst of being soothed and deeply aware of feelings of deep love for her family and the world of people, the farm, when all of a sudden she noticed a flash of brightness race across the dark-ridden fields. *Could that be a light from Jonathan's tractor*, she wondered watching the light disappear as if going onto the highway beyond the woods. *Where could he be going?*

On this night, Susanne Inverson and Jonathan Goodson found their way to this mysterious setting, and parked along the pond's bank. His arm is around her slender shoulders. "Susanne you're so lovely and engaging in the moonlit surroundings. "I love you, with all my heart. I love you."

"I love you, Jonathan," she said softly with deepest emotion, "I belong to you alone."

Soon they found themselves in the throes of sexual passion. In a husky voice, both helpless, over taken, told her, "I don't care if I do die; do die. I just want to let the juice fly, the juice fly." The couple's loud laughter echoed throughout the darkened surroundings.

Hello, I'm Susanne, from the Inverson farm. I'd like to welcome you to Penns Valley. Eric and I have the apple trees, and your name?" Tall, blond attractive Susanne Inverson smiling said, cuddling her cat, a beautiful, white fluffy tabby. Carol smiled introducing herself, and welcomed her neighbor inside the handsome, rambling two-story brick and wood frame house where the two visited, and got to know each other.

Susanne O Connor Inverson could never erase from her memory the stark poverty that had been deposited on her family when she was growing up. She and her siblings had known hunger intimately. Often, there was very little to eat, sometimes the cupboards were empty, and maybe a small portion of cheese was all that could be found in the icebox. And the family was forced to wear the tossed out clothes of others, from rummage sales or the Salvation Army usually. The second-hand clothing Susanne and the rest of the family never wore anything new, even down to their underwear. She would never forget how embarrassed she always was. At school she and her siblings were always looked down upon by the children at school because of the hand-me-down, ill-fitting things they wore. While she was still quite young, Susanne made a vow to herself that she wouldn't be impoverished like her parents, and began making plans to remove herself from the dire circumstances of her family. (As soon as she reached a legal age, she began taking on jobs as a store clerk or in offices working after school and weekends in order to buy and wear new and decent clothes. The ridicule stopped when she became quite a dresser, which improved her appeal tremendously. She had physical attractiveness-almost no one in her high school was more naturally beautiful.) And, sure enough, when she met Eric Inverson in High School-he was three years ahead of Susanne-she was almost certain that there lie great possibility for her destiny. When Susanne O'Connor married well to do Eric Inverson in 1970 it changed her destiny and everything in her life became much, much better.

Carol Goodson began to have suspicions about her husband and another woman. And she was right on target! The telephone would ring, and when she answered the person hung up. One evening everything came to the light. Carol was straightening things in their bedroom. She was inside a closet when she thought she heard husband Jonathan enter the room. The next thing she knew, he was heard using the telephone. Carol remained perfectly still and quiet as he began to speak with someone. She heard him say that he would meet the person, and he gave the specific location. Carol was destroyed; she felt her knees go weak, and had to put a hand over her mouth as she gasped. John left the house after hanging up. She knew the spot he'd mentioned. She waited a while before getting into her car. She was careful to stay out of view as she drove to the spot the rendezvous was taking place.

"Jonathan, bring your behind out of there!" Carol shouted from in front of the parking lot of a tavern in downtown Philadelphia. She'd gotten out of her car. Nothing happened. "I know you're in there with your whore Susanne Inverson!" Still no one came out. Anger pushed her to begin kicking his car. Then a volcano erupted in her and she went inside the tavern, spotted the two of them at a table, and went for Susanne, grabbing her by her long, blond hair. It would have filled her with pleasure to bang their heads together until their skulls were crushed into a fine powder. Carol seriously thought about gunning her pick-up, and ramming Susanne's up-scale home with the truck until she'd totally demolished her house. Nonetheless, Carol did nothing that evening, or at any other time. She came to realize something, that Susanne had done this to other women with their husbands.

An on-going affair had existed between Susanne and a Philadelphia politician among her other dalliances. As a matter of fact, without her knowing it, Carol once participated in an involvement. It seems Susanne came to Carol asking her to care for her treasured cat Timmy so she could attend to a very important matter. Her husband had travelled out of state for the week to an Agricultural conference. She told her she'd be gone for a couple of days and didn't want to leave Timmy alone in the house for that long a time.

As it turned out, Carol ran into a harrowing incident, and even injured herself while cat-sitting. Timmy got out of the house, and took off and ended up atop a fence. Trying to reach the pet, she fell onto the ground, and the fall injured her ankle. She managed to retrieve Timmy. He came out of the incident okay.

Carol thought she had a good neighbor and friend when she met Susanne Inverson. How wrong could she be!

The affair between Jonathan Goodson and Susanne Inverson actually began one afternoon when John had been trying to release one of his horses that managed to get away and got stuck in a muddy bank on her property, and she made her move. However it had all begun when he was building that boat for her husband, Eric. Working in their backyard, he had taken off his shirt, revealing his sinewy, glistening body. Susan had to have to restrain herself from going out there and propositioning him. She hadn't been able to release that sexy image from her mind.

Carol had answered the telephone when Susan Inverson called for Jonathan. Hard at work, he grumbled to his wife, saying to tell the neighbor he'd call when he'd finished.

"Jon, can you come over and check out my kitchen faucet. Our handyman is on vacation," she asked when he returned her call. He told her he'd be there as soon as he cleaned up a bit for he'd worked up quite a sweat. When he arrived and rang the doorbell Susanne met him wearing a sexy, black negligee. Embarrassed, he almost turned around to leave, thinking that she hadn't expected to see him at the front door. "I'm sorry, Mrs. Inverson. You're not dressed. I'm sorry. I should have gone to the back door, anyway." Jonathan couldn't have been more apologetic.

In her expertly smooth, sensual manner, Susan replied, "No need to be, Jonathan it's alright. As a matter of fact, it's fine; it's just the way that I planned it," she intoned, sexily, opening the door wider, and then stepped aside and with a sweep of her arm, invited him in. "I've been waiting for you, Jonathan. Come on in." As it turned out, she took him by the hand, leading him to her bedroom and her brand-new waterbed.

Did Eric Inverson's death happen because he'd grown tired of dealing with his wife's endless involvements with other men? If suicide caused his death, had her affair with Jonathan Goodson proved just too much to bear and he ended his life?

Apparently, Eric Inverson drowned in a creek. His tractor led police to his body face down in the creek near his property. On an extremely hot day had he gone there for a drink and heat exhaustion caused him to pass out, and he consequently drowned?

Mourners and curiosity seekers jammed Wright's Funeral Home. Eric Inverson's death had roused the farming community like nothing else. Local residents packed the small building. The rumor about Susanne's infidelity had been around for years. More than a few of the men had been her paramours which elevated the interest of everybody. Bernard remained beside his beloved Carol. He couldn't leave her there alone. It took every ounce of courage to keep from telling her how he wished everything could be different, and he could tell her how he felt about her. He so longed to have her with him. Susanne wept throughout the service; sometimes her gut-wrenching sounds filled the funeral home. Nobody there felt truth accompanied her cries of grief.

Chapter Ten

"I'd like to express my regret over the divorce. Know that I'm always here for you. You have my prayers, love, Bernard Willis." The note to Carol came with a dozen beautiful roses from her long-time friend. In return she sent him a letter thanking him for always remembering her, and being there for her with a genuine show of compassion. She wrote that he'd always been a sense of comfort as no one else. 'You're so strong and caring.' She never let him know it, but she also found him compelling and had to restrain herself for she wanted to throw herself into his arms and have him in a different and much deeper way. She'd always felt a sense of security, and when she was around him, it was where she wanted to remain forever. Everyone admired him. In their minds he was a giant for the way achieved and handled his marriage and dedication to his children.

"How nice,' she said out loud, "How nice." About two months after he sent the sympathetic message, Reverend Bernard Willis received an assignment to take over the ministry at a church in another state. He left with his family to serve a medium-sized congregation in Little Rock, Arkansas. From that point forward, he rose ever higher in the ministry and as a consequence, he and his family were often being moved about.

The popular recording playing at someone's wedding attracted most of the guests at someone's to the large dance floor. Anita couldn't help being drawn to tall, handsome, charming Martin Jackson; she had the same magnetic effect on him. And when the two met at the top of the dance line, they strolled together, each doing an impromptu dance intended to show off dancing ability at the wedding reception held at a fancy Philadelphia hotel. They tried to be discreet, but it was impossible for anyone not to know how powerful the feeling that existed between them.

"I want to see you. Write down your telephone number for me. I feel your magic, I can't resist you!" He'd whispered this to Anita. Eagerness exploded on her lovely face, and she smiled and nodded, yes. Both had come to someone's wedding with their mates, and had to exercise restraint and respect.

That dream was one of many Anita had about Martin Jackson.

In another dram about Martin Jackson, the two had left their mates to spend time together, and had ended up somewhere in a rundown section of New York City. Together again, sharing their love, happiness had claimed them. Anita once again had him and all of the wonderful experiences only Martin could give her. She even appreciated his displays of jealousy: would inquire about her every move, wanting to make certain that he was the only man in her life. In that dream he was oblivious to everything but her; senseless love had overtaken both of them. Recurrent in her dreams was the idea that he was obsessed with her, and he feared losing her. It seems he wanted to totally possess her. New York City always was a source of romance. From the time she was a small girl and learned about 'The Big Apple,' she'd romanticized: the vitality and energy of New York appealed like no other place on earth. In dreams, she often found herself somewhere in New York City, usually though, lost. Once she was in a strange parking lot trying to get to a high-rise building in downtown Manhattan for an appointment with a very important party. Strangely, she found herself in another dream, in this exact location, lost, at this parking lot, needing to get to an apartment where someone awaited her arrival. She would open up the shutters on the shadows over her life, and enjoy glorious, illustrious memories, or marvelous dreams that brought Martin Jackson and her together.

At first the dreams about Martin Jackson baffled her, but eventually she began to see that these dreams signified something important to her life. She couldn't stop fantasizing about him. His affect was so powerful that he would remain in her forever. She could be anywhere and he would become the subject of her thoughts, filling her up with more wonder and magic she once felt at a fairground as a child. Even though Anita was only dreaming about Martin Jackson, in reality feelings of passion toward him were so strong that she couldn't resist having his place in her thoughts and life.

"The crush of life pounds my heart, I

seek the living blood and guts

of forsaken love…life's true spirit.

The haunted soul has strayed in areas-antici-

pating the heap and heft of living to come

and conquer all of me, in my desperate

search for the freed spirit.

In experience' corners, I've felt its wealth

and worth, and saw beyond all that it has for me…

Before I lose the pearl hailing me with romance

and serenades, I'm wistful elusion is not a fixture,

with discovery joining happiness and

the freed spirit and me."

Martin Jackson stood before the black group of Black elites assembled at an NAACP event, smoothly reciting from one of his books. Anita sat breathless in the seaside resort roundhouse gripped by his smooth, inspiring poetic delivery. When he finished, he proceeded to deliver a talk about this marvelous site on the New Jersey shore that catered to the upper class, to which families as his belonged as did the Ramsey's.

"As everyone in this roundhouse knows, in the late 1940's a time when white resorts refused to admit Negroes, a handful of prosperous

Negroes purchased the idyllic property. The residents have always been what we have here: doctors, attorneys, funeral directors, educators, and others in upstanding professions, northeast residents from Philadelphia, New Jersey and New York. They found the rustic bayside resort ideal for leisure, rest and tranquility. (The preserve with its brooding, motionless, solemn atmosphere cast a hypnotic trance and provided boating, swimming, barbecues and many other recreational activities, the perfect playground for the families and their guests. It could be said about this location that the pristine, natural environment that it was serene as though it shared a universal spirit and an eternal silence harbored by the estuaries, seas oceans, inlets lakes, ponds which lapped the shores: it appeared regenerative elements saturated the surroundings).

The residences, mostly rustic cottages made of stucco, concrete, vinyl-sided, wood, and insignificant in appearance, they served extravagantly with relaxation and calm. (Inhabitants were unrestrained, and had stocked their dwelling with everything in good measure for relaxation and comfort-clothing, reading material, music, food stuffs, everything, including ample supplies of fine liquors).

"The exclusive Black idyllic bayside resort to this day is gives pleasure to about a hundred summer residents of enormous status and privilege. Some of these professionals have family connections to heroes from the American Revolution and Civil War or with Blacks in the vanguard of social and economic change in America, or descended from Freed Men.

Indeed, this particular resort became a natural setting for a highbred Negro society-African Americans of influence and prominence-a location where they could experience leisure and the good life."

"This particular resort cradled its residents with pleasure and leisure and the rhapsodic song of summer. Daytime throbbed with recreation on the sun-beaten water or campgrounds-boating, swimming, cookouts, softball, cards, parlor games. As darkness fell, solitude and magic overspread the environment. The cresting, rapturous Bay thrashed against the shore with mortal silence, and the surroundings succumb to a passionate, mystical, phantasmagoric darkness. The inhabitants cloistered in the cottages pursuing some gratifying activity. Or they took off for restaurants or nightclubs. During the earlier times a policy of discrimination meant that it was likely they would not be served if they went to the ones nearby. In this case they drove the thirty or so miles into Atlantic City. The Negro clubs in Atlantic City always had top entertainers-Billy Eckstein, Sarah Vaughn, Duke Ellington, Lionel Hampton, Joe Williams, Billy Holiday and a host of others." Applause filled the roundhouse. Then Martin Jackson, smiling told the group:

"One more poem, and I'm done this evening. Thank you for being such a generous audience."

I wander through wanderlust with silky smoothness that resides

with floral beauty, tranquilizing breezes, and the breathless loveliness

in all other wonders of nature and life.

All hope is love stored as a mystical image, forlorn, waiting to empty into the

dark forest of the mind/heart/soul. Intimidation wraps itself around us as we stumble

through life unaware.

Anita couldn't stop the strong desire to be with Martin Jackson once he'd shown up in her life. She noticed the enormous longing while doing almost anything.

It had all begun during the time she was chauffeuring her sons Billy and Albert to Little League practices or as she sat in front of the country club waiting to pick them up from a Boy Scout meeting. She met Martin Jackson, waiting for his ten-year-old son, Martin Jr., a member of her son's scouting program. The two parents sat side by side on a bench as they waited in the lobby.

It became a need to feast on the tall, dark-skinned handsome, beautiful speaking man, a need as deep and constant as a craving. His presence carried her to a starry, heavenly place. She felt cozy, embraced and transported, as you would experience through beautiful pieces of art and photography.

"Basically I am a poet, familiar with the outskirts of life, plus existing with immense desolation. And, I have had the marvelous experience of being in the palm of the open sky. I like to look into the sanctuary of nature, to that place which survives beyond view. There is in the memory of everybody's time a place lost, and rediscovered, and I enjoy peering into that sacred, hallowed ground. Simplicity, peace and serenity bound up, persuade and enrich my spirit, aiming me toward a place of permanence and restfulness, although I can only glimpse and savor its vision for me. Back to the subject, 'celebrities,' I don't give a whole lot of praise to stars, entertainers, high-powered politicians and other limelighters. I applaud the common people, those who have to struggle with life. Kudos goes to the average woman with children as she juggles children, a household and career. With the kind of assistance celebrity mothers enjoy-nannies, cooks, housekeepers, and the rest-it'll be the normal working mother homemaker I will highly regard every time."

"Arthur Jackson, my father has worked for years as a US mail carrier for the city of Chicago Post Office. I always admired my father even though he didn't seem to see himself in the way I and most saw him. I had much admiration for this man who possessed much more than his average education. Nonetheless he was guarded, insecure and even suspicious. He was strong but was out of touch with just how many strengths he possessed. I think he had filed away hurtful memories from the past and didn't judge himself with an open mind. He grew up in. segregated Mississippi, and worked hard from his earliest years alongside of his siblings and parents on the family farm. "Hee ah! Hee ah! Whumpa!" nine-year-old Arthur Bradley ordered his two mule team right and left, as he steered, with precision, the two husky animals down a row of cotton.

"My wife, Janice is Korean. A loving Caucasian couple adopted her at four-years-old from a Korean orphanage. The owner of a successful brick building business and his wife of many years were a loving, devout Christian couple. With Judith as their daughter the couple felt that they couldn't have asked for more. Janice couldn't have had life better than the loving, solid Christian home Susanne and George Anderson provided. She had the best of everything she needed and more.

"I was just completing my degree in Law at the University of Pennsylvania when Janice Anderson made her entrance into my life. That day I saw the most beautiful girl I'd ever seen walking across the University of Pennsylvania campus with an armload of books. I just had to get to know her. Everything I saw called out to me: she was tall, slender with long lustrous black hair bouncy hair. I sped up my stroll.

"Could you please slow down for just a moment? I'm not in as good shape as you," I smilingly said, hoping she'd stop when I caught up. Up close her Asian sleek, almond-shaped eyes and everything else increased her beauty. I felt my heart skip when she gave me a smile that said she was willing to give me a chance." Anita listened, mesmerized, wishing she'd been Janice.

Martin Jackson, a successful attorney, and Janice Anderson Jackson as heart surgeon attained prominence.

****

On this warm fall afternoon Anita Ramsey and Martin Jackson sat together on a bench outside the country club in the sun shining brilliantly, as they for their sons when the Boy Scout meeting ended.

"What a luxury it is to look out at the sky, and focus on cloud formations," Martin Jackson said, wanderlust tracing his smile. She sat there eager for a poetic presentation and the sense of wistfulness it would engender. "I like to take unbeaten paths. Janice, Martin Jr. and I once took a trip to North Carolina, and I just decided we'd try a Bed and Breakfast instead of the usual hotels. I can tell you, it turned out to be a marvelous experience for my family and me. We trampled in some nearby woods, strolled along a lonely lakeside beach, and enjoyed wonderful food and service at the modest, warm, friendly home for four days. We had an incredible time."

Anita smiled, waiting for what he'd lift next out of his poetic passages for her exhilaration. She felt her heart rising as she listened to this man who seemed to reside in a broad spectrum, a universal spirit.

"I remember once as a teen working as a waiter in an upscale restaurant, the very first African American employed there. One night, my second evening, a White ritzy couple and their small child, a blond beautiful girl around three years old were having dinner. The husband, wife and little girl seemed pleasant enough. However, after they'd finished, their paid bill on the table, "Here's something for you," the man smiling said, as he handed me something, an object of some kind. Now, chuckling, and seeming in a hurry to leave, he ushered his family away. When I looked at the unfamiliar thing in my hand I was baffled. Later, I learned from my parents that it was a JuJu doll. That racist bastard gave me a JuJu doll!"

"What's a JuJu doll," Anita asked, totally unfamiliar. He smiled and explained to her about the racism the object implied.

Anita's heart pounded with happiness to be with him and his family, at such a location. *How did I come to find myself in a mix such as this*, she thought when she awoke. And, she wondered why she could feel such compassion toward this writer, this poet who haunted her in dreams.

Anita and Carol had become very sensitive and sympathetic personalities as result of their experiences throughout their lives, being racially mixed, and their appearance showed it. They'd been taunted and ridiculed, and shown animosity and unacceptance throughout their lives in one way or another. Principally, the worst experience had come from girls of color who out of jealousy harassed them. From those times, and others the two sisters developed a deep sense of compassion for others.

In one of Anita's many particular luxurious dreams, a dark haven of night had fallen over their two houses, the bungalow Martin Jackson and his wife lived in, and her own. The small homes had a set of steps of no more than two feet of space between them. Everything the scenario appeared simple but at the same time capable of indulging her with romance. He crossed the barrier between them and entered her home and provided her everything she'd missed without him in her life, and met all of her sensual needs.

"Martin, I love you so…." she woke up in the middle of the night, hearing herself say.

****

Martin Jackson's entry into Anita Ramsey's life was magical; it seemed his presence had been something for which she'd always yearned. Once, she was at a pool party at the lovely home of her brother Jimmy. It was a large, marvelous house in a gated community, outside of Philadelphia nestled in a marvelous thicket. Her brother and his wife Judy and their two young daughters were hosting a family get-together. Her mother Julia plus aunts, uncles and cousins, and other relatives and friends were there. A Saturday in late-July could have been scorching hot, uncomfortable. However, it was not; coolness was at the base of the warm atmosphere and was felt embracing the breeze. (The mid-summer day was perfect for swimming, not too warm or chilly).

Music was coming from the CD player was mostly jazz and rhythm and blues, and was smoothing out the experience for everyone swimming or poolside in lounge chairs around the piano-shaped pool in light, happy conversation. Sounds of Quincy Jones vibrant, exciting music was most compatible for setting the stage for the outdoor, poolside gathering. This was a luscious event. She was ever so grateful to be there for she felt more collected and calm than she had for quite some time. She was always in the mid-stream of something ruinous or bordering on disaster; her life was almost never as calm as this. Her mind was spiraling with a section of life pulled away from a visit she'd recently made to the Frederick Douglass museum. The great African American's summer home, turned museum was in a gated-community called Highland Venice Beach, a seductive, exclusive site along the Chesapeake Bay. She'd been considering doing a biography of the famous African American. She was seduced by the naturalness and serene woods encircling her brother, Jimmy's Tuscan-style home. Anita had found herself recreating that visit. When she and the others were making the trek through the sandy roads along the Chesapeake Bay toward the summer home of the Abolitionist, writer, nineteenth-century international African American figure, Fredrick Douglas a treasured solitude and enthusiasm seemed to accompany the people comprising the small troupe. Once the energetic troupe of people had entered the two-story wood frame, porch house, the group was captivated by a time honored still and reverence which encapsulated the house. (A relaxing, soothing quality, a solemn spirit from the past exalted throughout and there was the sense and sensation that the area was blanketed by that honored past, and was stilling everything. Every object and artifact left in the deeply quiet rooms of the summer home increased the wondrous, reminiscent effect of the site created for the elevated guests who once assembled there).

Chapter Eleven

Carol had trouble adjusting to life after the divorce. Nearly a year later and she struggled with hurt and disappointment over the failed marriage. Sadly, she all she could think about was how much she thought they'd shared over the three years they'd been together. She also felt deeply having experienced the tragedy of losing their two children, and never enjoying parenthood. Most of all, she hadn't got over her love for him. *How did things go awry? How did it come to this?* Over and over, she sadly asked herself. She'd had such beautiful dreams about love, and the man she'd married. She assumed Jonathan than man she'd waited to discover her. In a dream she often had, she'd become a singer/performer. One evening as she performed on stage, singing lovely, enchanting pop and some opera songs, he had a front row seat in the audience. She noticed him the entire time, looking at her with love coming from him to her on stage. When she'd finished for the evening, he'd come back stage and they embraced, and knew in that instant they were meant to be together in love. They'd run off together to New York City to live happily ever after.

****

"Much as you wonder about things, you probably even though ole Leroy coulda been your father," Julia Bernstein broke out laughing at the absurdity of her statement. Carol couldn't help laughing as well. Leroy Jones was hired to help run the farm when her ex Jonathan left the household. A cripple, Leroy was in his middle to late sixties. A diminutive man, with a slight build, Leroy Jones was deeply dark skin with broad, Negroid features, sparse kinky hair. He wore clothes that were baggy as though a larger person had once worn them. Generally, he was dependable and hardworking, took pride in his work, and was always eager to please. With his gleeful eyes and likeable personality, Leroy Jones became someone Carol and Julia were glad to have around. However, he could be quite the prankster. ("I'm just going to the tavern for a while, Miss Carol and Miss Julia." The two women would respond, giving their assent. Leroy never left the farm. He would hang around under the windows and make wild animal sounds. When they were sufficiently frightened, he run into the house, prepared to assist. Carol and Julia were going along with the hireling to whom they referred to as 'Little Man' to please him).

The hunchback came to have deep meaning to Carol. He loved the tall coconut cake Julia often made for him and the peas and okra dish she fixed and served with corn meal muffins. They did all kinds of special things for Leroy. Around the two women, the crippled drifter was totally happy. The cripple hireling was a likeable, dependable person, although he seemed bound by aloneness and some remoteness. Carol felt guilty she hadn't advanced her life, and shown them they'd been the best parents anyone could have. Leroy Jones' humble presence could lift her from her feelings of heartbreak and sorrow. With all of his honest, kind and amicable qualities, he was certainly not pitiable or invisible. Nothing could detract from this magnificent little man. Carol and her mother Julia cast off his handicap as if it were a coat; his physical condition only served to embolden him, and he shone like a brilliant, beckoning light.

Among the vivid impressions Carol would receive about her parents, the one from which she could not budge, and had the most impact involved the two people meeting at a small, dingy roadside café, situated off of a major highway in the area. The dim-lit nightspot attracted a regular crowd. Most were Negroes who worked at the local industries; it drew a small number of Hispanic workers in the vicinity as well-on weekends the crowd grew so large that people spilled outside the club in the parking lot. Another scenario about her parents had them meeting one evening during a bad storm. The two met when both took shelter in a flea market held in a tired-looking red barn to escape the pouring rain. Carol couldn't figure out what had attracted her father and her mother to each other. But she was really hopeful that their experience was more than just a crossing of paths.

Chapter Twelve

"Anita, this is something both of us need, a picnic together." Eddie Ramsey said this nodding as together they spread out the blanket on the park grounds. His comment baffled her, and she looked at him with a wondering look. *Has he some suspicion about me and my interest in Martin Jackson?* Although she knew that infidelity hadn't taken place with her and Martin Jackson the charming poet, she had to admit the two had been seeing each other, and being with him brought her joyous feelings.

"I welcome this, sweetheart. We have been spending less time together, without the boys. And, it feels good just to have ourselves for a change."

"Yes, I sort of thought we'd drifted apart, and maybe we should focus on our relationship like we used to." He smiled and pulled her down on the blanket and pulled her to him, and they wrapped themselves in an embrace.

****

"What's this?" Anita asked herself, lifting a letter from an envelope she'd found in her husband, Eddie's jacket pocket. "Who's this woman Salome Ughani? She's saying what here? What's been going on?" In the letter Salome Ughani meant to regain contact with Eddie Ramsey. It seems this woman, Salome Ughani husband's recent death started her to think about the love she and Eddie Ramsey had shared all those years ago. She wanted to get to see him again, see if they could restart the love they let go of.

What does this mean? Anita worriedly asked herself.

Anita decided that a trip to England would serve as a reprieve from the daily agony with which she'd been living since she discovered that her husband Eddie was seriously involved with another woman.

Anita and a small group she was with had just left Westminster Abbey, and were now about to board a riverboat on the Thames River. "How could Arthur deceive me this way? And I thought I accounted for any seams in our marriage. I never imagined he could be involved in any way," Anita despondently thought, tears dripping from the striking azure-blue eyes of the tall, blond, svelte, stylish middle-age attractive woman. On this the 21st day of September, 2001, for three days she'd been in London, England staying at the Regency. "Jim, I haven't been able to contact you. What's going on? I haven't been able to make contact with the boys either since I've been here. Please let me know something." Rosalyn placed her cell phone back into her purse, and continued with tourists boarding the boat.

"Hello, darling, are you certain the job will get done? This would not have been the route I'd take but I'll go along with whatever it takes to become Mrs. Cynthia Ramsey. Yes, darling I understand what you're saying, that a divorce from Anita would strap us. Well, if this is what we have to do, get rid of our mates, it's what we shall do. Call me the moment you hear that the job is done, my darling."

"Welcome, everyone, welcome aboard the Thames River boat ride. You'll get to view much of London's great sites!" The boat conductor dressed as a ship captain was a middle-aged man of medium height and slender with a long, gaunt face and swarthy complexion. She realized that was the same man who beckoned from a door at Westminster Abbey, but she could only guess he'd waved to the other tourists. Something about the conductor was unsettling; it seemed to he concealed something sinister. The thought that he resembled Charon at the River Styx was chilling.

The solo seven-day trip was meant to regenerate her enough to help her make clear what to do about her marriage and her life. Arthur, "Cynthia and I are not having an affair." His response didn't stop her feelings about her husband and his secretary Connelly. He'd refused marital counseling saying: "Why would we get counsel when nothing's wrong?" She came to think that if nothing else, a trip away from everything might clear her head.

"Welcome aboard the ferryboat ride along the Thames!" announced the eerie-looking conductor sitting next to the rail of the 22-foot boat. When all of the tourists were seated, the conductor turned his attention toward Anita with a crafty smile that made her feel uneasy. Turning away from him to look at the river, terror seized her to see ghostly images rising from the dark surging waters, reaching out to her, making horrifying moaning, lusty sounds. The Thames soon became an upheaval with ghosts tearing away at her flesh, groaning with satisfaction for a dinner the ferryboat captain had promised.

Anita awoke perspiring profusely and frightened out of her mind. *I have to ask him what that letter is all about.*

****

"I found this letter as I was cleaning out your pocket jacket to take it to the cleaners. Who's this woman who says she still loves you? According to this letter, it seems her husband's death she wants you back. What's this all about?"

"Anita, I apologize. I should've destroyed that letter when it arrived two weeks ago. It means nothing to me, she means nothing to me. I have not responded because I am content with my life with you and our sons. I can tell you this, years ago she mattered. Years ago, long before I met and fell head over hills for you, I was a young man who fell in love with a married, older woman. But believe me, after I met you, all of my feelings for her went away, and I loved only you, you and you alone." She smiled and told him, she understood. He reached for her and with her close, they kissed deeply. He lifted her into his arms, and kissing her, he carried her to the deep expressions of love that awaited them in the sanctity of the bedroom.

All the while ferocious love-making took place she had feelings of guilt over her attraction to Martin Jackson.

Chapter Thirteen

"Eddie, I'd like to find Gilbert Johnson, and kill that S.O.B," Elva said with deep anger contorting her face. He don't deserve to live after the suffering and abuse he caused me family all those years. The only good that came out of all of it, is Boo, my child that I love more than anything on earth." She wanted to tell him that she cared almost as much for him. "I'm glad though that the bastard's no longer around my younger sisters to do what he did to me. I sometimes feel guilty that I didn't report him, take the chance, put him to the test about his threats to kill us all if told anyone. But I didn't, and my young sister, Angela did what I didn't have the nerve to do. Thank God she told me what he tried to do to her but she managed to prevent him by yelling out to my mother. The bastard ran out of the house, and ain't been seen since. I just hope somebody reports him, and the Law catch him, and make him pay for everything, all of the damage he's done to my family, and probably other. I just hope that he's not able to do this to anybody else, wherever he is. As far as I know, he's still out there."

"You know, I suspected him, when you told me you'd become pregnant with Boo, and preferred not to tell me how it happened. We'd always shared everything, and I couldn't understand why you'd withhold that from me," Eddie Ramsey told her, his voice filled with sadness and regret.

Thinking it not the right time, she didn't mention her pregnancy. He'd attended to her as he always had when he heard about Jack's death. But, she just didn't want to confess to someone living such a respectful as Eddie Ramsey.

****

"We're the Seattle Police with a warrant for the arrest of, Gilbert Johnson," the mammoth white officers told the eighty-seven-year-old, frail-looking Caucasian woman holding onto to a walker at the door of the large, beautiful house.

"He works for me. He lives on my property me, doing things for me around the home and property. He lives in that shed over there," she weakly, nervously informed the two policemen, pointing to an outbuilding.

The two lawmen, nodded and, thanked the frightened woman, and headed for the small building that served as Gilbert Johnson's living quarters. The law officers did not find him there and so they left. That very day, Elva's brother discovered Gilbert's whereabouts. He'd been pushed by anger for the life Gilbert had shoved on him and his siblings and their mother. However his real reason for hunting Gilbert Johnson stemmed from an account of his youngest sister, when she finally opened up about the sexual abuse she'd suffered, and kept silent about all of that time. From that point on, he'd been searching, searching for the man that had wounded his family, and mainly his siblings.

That late evening, Gilbert answered his small cottage door before he knew what to expect. He neither knew about the police and the arrest, earlier, or anything. To his surprise, Elva's brother John assassinated him on the spot, shooting him as many times as his gun would let him. Instantly, Gilbert fell in the tiny doorway, dead.

****

Particles of light solidified a zone of comfort around Anita and husband Eddie, and the couple's two young sons, Eddie Jr and Paul. Anita Ramsey felt content as never before having such a sound, loving and extremely happy family. The most startling and fascinating of all about being with her husband included their regular torrid love-making. Together they were outstanding, emotionally and physically she was in a marvelous place she'd never known as they shared caring and tender relationship. He touched off sensuous feelings she never knew existed inside of her. She never stopped pinching herself over everything that had taken place in her life, the happiness that filled her life. 'Why then did she have these romantic notions about Martin Jackson', she had to ask herself.

"I'll teach those boys of yours how to climb a tree the way I taught my boy, the way my father taught me." The two sat side by side on the sofa together, she secure and blissful in the clutches of his strong arm. Everything had worked out as she'd imagined. Her assumptions about Martin Jackson had been right, he could be amazing with her sons; maybe even do better than their own father, who'd showed them how to play softball, football, and basketball, plus engage in other sports and activities. She smiled listening, smiling as he in his beautiful manner of speech described all of the things they would do together to become a solid, healthy, happy family.

The night was majestic, rich and dark, with a host of glittering stars. Rugged waves banged against the sandy shore, rebounded and softly made their way back into the endless ocean. The dark-ladled night was caressing and soft with love as she and Martin Jackson strolled hand in hand along Cole Cove Beach, Florida. The couple was headed for the shore to be near the ocean and be alone with time and the universe and love. She'd left John Jr., Robert and Charles with a sitter back at the quaint Atlantic Hotel where the four had been staying. A summer vacation couldn't have been more fulfilling, for her and him, and her two boys as well. Their days began with a marvelous breakfast at the hotel's outdoor restaurant, and then a spectacular day at the beach. Afterwards, they returned to the hotel to change for dinner, and chose a restaurant more wonderful than the one the evening before.

She awoke from that dream smiling, and yearning to see him.

****

"Elva, you have to hold on, please, don't leave Boo and me and others who love you," Carol begged in the ICU where Elva was slipping away, she and the baby at risk of dying. Her pregnancy had come with serious complications. Sadly, she developed pre-eclampsia-gestational hypertension. The disease put her life and her baby's at great risk. Now, during delivery, death seemed imminent.

"Carol, it don't look good for me and this baby. I don't think we're gonna make it. I'm gonna ask you a huge favor, I wouldn't ask anybody else this. But can I ask you to look after Boo, in the event we don't make it?" With tears seeping, Elva weakly turned her face away from her dearest friend. "I wouldn't want Boo, or anything of mine to have anything to do with my family"

"You're going to be okay, you and that baby, stop talking nonsense. Nothing's going to happen, and if did, you wouldn't have had to ask. I'd step in whether I'd been asked or not," she tearfully replied.

****

Elva Davis had died delivering a child she named Sharon before she took her last breath. The funeral took place at St. Luke Episcopal Church in Philadelphia. Deep, overwhelming sorrow had everyone in its grip. Eddie Ramsey managed to have the funeral for his sister-in-law Carol's best friend at his family's church. Eddie and Anita Ramsey and their sons entered the church and sat in the pew just behind Carol, with the newborn Sharon in her arms, and Boo sitting beside her. As he sat down, Eddie reached put his hand gently into Carol's hand, then shook Boo's hand. Anita leaned forward and kissed her sister's cheek, and also gave Boo a kiss.

A large number attended the home-going in support of Elva and her children. Her large family had the run-down look of folks who'd lived hard, callous, unproductive urban lives. They even looked the part by their inappropriate dress: what they had on looked more like something you'd wear to a night-club, or to a family barbeque. They tried appearing sorrowful, but they couldn't turn to deep feelings they didn't possess. A long-time separation had removed them from an emotional connection-they'd stopped giving her existence much consideration since she'd left to be on her own all those years ago. Harriet, Elva's mother, sobbing quietly, sorrowfully showed lots of aging, but didn't appear terribly beat-up considering her lifestyle, and all she'd been through.

****

Carol couldn't have felt lower in her life as when she signed the papers legally divorcing her from Jonathan. She now had twelve-year-old Boo. She was happy to know that young Boo loved the farm environment, and didn't have to make any adjustment to life around him. Naturally, her love for that child began from the time he and his mother came into her life. She had his and Baby Sharon's futures in her hands. She had every intention of providing everything they would need to insure them a good life.

"Carol, will you become my wife?" Bernard Willis earnestly asked.

"Yes, I will, Bernard my love, absolutely, yes," she responded, looking deeply into the most loving, sincere eyes she'd ever seen.

Chapter Fourteen

Who could have imagined that something that meant so much to Anita would come crashing to an end.

Martin Jackson always enjoyed the peaceful environment at his retreat in West Haven Connecticut. It seemed to wash away all of his concerns; he always returned to Philadelphia revived and ready to deal with Court Justice. Four years before, he and his wife had instantly purchased the modest three-bedroom wood frame in this little tranquil section off of Long Island Sound. The house was anything but spectacular, but it met their desires. Maybe it satisfied the family because you had only to make ten steps or less to get to the sandy beach.

In 1980, Martin Jackson went there in the last stages of sickle cell disease that had dominated his entire life, and there he left this world.

When Anita got the tragic news, she almost collapsed. She knew she could never put Martin Jackson out of her life. To express her deep, deep grief, tearfully and sorrowfully she wrote the following poem

Since you're gone, my life is cold as snow.

In this sad heart no warmth can flow…

Can't you come back to me?……

Darkness is my only view…….

Light could only come from you….

Can't you come back to me?…..

If you returned you'd move away this

endless eventide………..

You would bring waves of joy to fill an ocean wide…

My heart's empty without you….

With you gone I feel so blue….

Can't you come back to me?..

Come back to me, come back to

me and stay….

For months and beyond, she had dreams about him.

"Hey, it's me, can I meet you some place? I miss you so much I have to see you, Anita. Name the place and I'll get there,"

"Where ever you say I'll be there," Anita told him, joy pumping her heart hearing his voice.

"Why don't you come to me, that might be the best thing to do," he slurred, filled with excitement over the idea that he'd get to see her.

Anita couldn't wait to get into her car and start for the spot they'd agreed to meet. In about half an hour she'd come to the New Jersey turnpike, headed for the first rest stop there. As soon as she pulled onto the parking lot, she became breathless with excitement as he climbed out of his car to come her way. Seeing his tall, lanky image once again took her breath away. He seemed as real as the last time she'd seen him just before his death. With renewing interest, dreams such as this one kept coming about Martin Jackson. It seemed he'd never left her life.

"When I spotted a mansion in the distance and began pushing through the heavy dark ocean even harder, feeling I had a chance to survive. I hear music of Hayden, Bach, Liszt, Sibelius, Revell, Schubert, Mozart and other classical composers the magnificent sound lifts me and transport my spirit toward elevated environs; I am reaching at strains and strands of glorious, joyous life. The experience is unattainable, intangible, renewing: the marvelous music blissfully filters into my soul.

I had no idea about the lovely sprawling home, just knew that it offered hope. The boat had overturned and I found myself in the Atlantic Ocean fearful and cold.

How did I arrive at this strange place in front of me, she wondered , confused as she began to climb up the bank toward the magnificent home and gala going on. *What could this mean, why have I come to this particular place? Has someone invited me?* Then, she wondered if I could have become swept up in a dream, a dream of yearning unfulfilled?

"Welcome, my beloved, with bated breath I've been waiting for you," as he took her hand in his, and ushered her inside of wide window-pane doors, toward the shining glamourous activity of people on the ballroom floor dancing to the beautiful music.

"Martin, it's you. Is this a dream, or am I seeing you again?"

"Where are you, my Poet? You took me down a path of mystery, inspiration, and love. I miss your presence." She picked up one of his books and began experiencing him, the only connection, the only thing she knew to do for comfort:

Thirty-five-year-old, African American William Lowell could swear he'd mistakenly hit the button on his car radio, and changed the station, the reason for the light classical music playing all of a sudden. A musician classically trained, he recognized the music softly playing in his car came from eighteenth-century composer Mozart. The incident became more strange however as he remembered when the happening took place. He'd just crossed the line from Pennsylvania into northern Delaware, and realized a transformation, when the surroundings seemed to take on a different appearance, a look that seemed to go backward in time. Somehow, everything he saw along the Back Bay, the northern tract in Delaware seemed to have ramifications that a natural change had occurred. "Have I made a wrong turn and got off my route?" he asked himself, feeling totally out of place.

Everything he witnessed in the environs as he drove seemed different, fuller than he remembered. And it felt as if life had slowed, and almost motionless: Wildlife Park, Bombay Hook, Port Mahon, Grass Dale, Little Creek, wetlands, woods, flowers, fauna, fields, sights and sounds. In an area of countryside a darkly-shrouded grassy knoll could have represented a location for Don Quixote of La Mancha to at any moment appear on his scrawny horse Docinante, and begin attacking windmills he mistook for armies.

In the solemn Back Bays he felt aware of an eerie presence of the early British who settled the region. Folklore and mystery seemed carried on the wind in an atmosphere that revitalized the original settlers fishing villages, old taverns, cattails, and an amazing grandiloquent 1700's manor.

I think I'll stop in this old tavern, since it looks as if it's open to the public, and find out where I am, William Lowell thought, as he drove onto the tavern grounds. Once he'd opened the heavy wooden door, and stepped inside, he wondered what was going on. Everyone there could have been actors in a movie or a stage production the way they looked, dressed in period clothing. The men and a couple of barmaids all appeared to have stepped out of Colonial America.

"Sir, what can I serve ya?" the man behind the wooden counter asked William as he approached the bar.

"Could you tell me if this is some theatre group being video-taped?" William asked, shaking his head baffled beyond belief.

"What, sir, are you saying?" the bartender earnestly inquired with a quizzical stare. "By the way, sir, why are dressed that way? Why does everyone look so strange? What is this place?

Deeply disturbed by everything he saw, William quickly decided he had no reason to remain in such a perplexing situation, he left tavern with hope he'd find a way back to reality.

Outside and getting in his car, he realized the sharp strains of eighteenth-century classical music had resumed. As he drove feeling lost and confused, something caused him to relate the strange occurrence at the tavern to his family, the Lowell's when as a small boy he visited his grandparent's mammoth house in a very old, elevated section in Philadelphia. Every time he went into a particular darkened corridor of that house, what he encountered always frightened him. He'd see apparitions of nineteen-century women, deceased relatives. The women wore high-collared long dresses, high-buttoned shoes, and they had their hair pulled back in chignons, buns, or twists. They never said a word as they came into the long dark hall from rooms. *Perhaps that house was haunted, and the tavern haunting and it might be related,* he thought as he tried to figure out where he was, and how to get to his home in Delaware to his wife, Clara and their three children Thomas, Mary and Williams Jr.

Anita took a pause from reading for a moment, realizing the sense of comfort and hope of Martin Jackson's legacy. Smiling, she resumed reading.

This particular inlet is a desolate, ominous place with unremitting silence, and where the stench of death and decay fills the atmosphere.

It is an evening in spring, the time when the Horseshoe crab comes to the Delaware shores to spawn and die. (The Horseshoe crab is a seafaring creature with a spiked head and a tank-like body and resembles a Viking in armor.) The path to the inlet follows a narrow, dirt road flocked by tall, ink-tipped bulrush and sedge through tall fields of wheat, barley and corn.

"The ancient bodies of the Horseshoe crab cram the inlet's dark, murky waters and the pebbly shores are crowded with their carcasses. (It is a clamorous event with hundreds swimming, and clamoring to join Horseshoe crab that number in the thousands cluttering the stony beach).

A frail wooden pier stands a short distance away in the middle of the dark, active, dramatic waters. (The frail wooden pier seems to be a scale for the desertion of life, a helpless structure there in the passive surreal drape covering the environment of the inlet. Inexplicably, the pier site turns my thoughts to shipwrecks, pirates' coves, coral reefs and even to damask tablecloths). Nevertheless, the fragile pier is imperturbable, a kind of universal resistance standing there, with natural grace affirming it.

The isolated inlet seems to have journeyed from the moon, the cosmos, or some archaic isle or even Pluto's Hell to claim this eternal location.

A spirit of classicism elevates the historical environs of "The Green" through the magnificent, glorious music of Bach, Beethoven, Liszt, Mozart, Schubert and other great classical composers. The atmosphere is almost electric with a renewing, joyousness you experience with the marvelous music filtering into your senses.

In Dover, Delaware's Capital, where the first signing of the United States Constitution took place December 7, 1787, it seems a wall of Grace and permanence has partitioned that historic area identified as, "The Greens." The impact of Dover's historical inheritance hovers across "The Green," the seat of Government as a realm of a prevailing light composing Legislative Hall and a State House and other early municipal buildings. In the area amid and the verdant foliage surroundings you have Christ Episcopal Church in Dover, established in 1734, Barratt's Chapel near Frederica, Delaware, given the title, 'The Cradle of Methodism' in America, to name just some of the early ecclesiastical influences.

Summarizing "The Greens'" surroundings, you experience a Revolutionary spirit, and as well an Anglican reverence in the atmosphere. You become aware of a 'Protestant' adherence bearing down with a sense of calm, reassurance, contentment and high regard for guarded conduct. It seemed the influence of Wasp orthodoxy expanded the atmosphere with a bell-piercing transcendent, classical sentience over "The Greens."

Delaware's State Seal comprises a sheaf of wheat, an ear of corn and an ox symbolizing early farming. The State Flag of Delaware incorporates the seal's images along with the date "December 7, 1787," showing that Delaware was the first state to ratify the United States Constitution.

The Town Hall, a Colonial structure constituted an honorable, revitalizing force. A Georgian, brick façade, the historic building had accommodated America's beginnings-it engaged some of the earliest colonialists in discussions establishing America. The Town Hall represented a time-honored historic municipal building as other Corinthian, Ionic structures across America.

Delaware State College and Wesley College, both located in the city of Dover, stoutly served the state in higher education. In the city of Dover the Agricultural Museum, a large barn-styled building stored and displayed the life of the farming community.

Located in the obscurity of rural Delaware, the town hall of magnificence and splendor might have surpassed the lot of colonial municipalities reflecting the earliest staging of America. Though moderate in size, the structure had immense bearing and was a stalwart representation of its natural origins. However, beyond the patriotic significance emanating from the town hall, a universal boundary circumscribed it, and massed by darkness, it was a glittering diamond, a small wonder. It was a municipality amassed by darkness, a gem…a glittering diamond.

A statue of an ink well and quill honors the first state to sign the document ratifying the United States. The ink well and quill, inscribed with, "Dover's Gift to America," sits on a promontory in the area of "The Greens". It symbolizes the freedom and liberty attained when the Colonies signed the Constitution after the long War defeating English rule.

A sight common on streets, roads and highways in the area presents the solemn dark image of a horse and buggy with an Amish family inside.

Kent and Sussex Counties back then presented a landscape producing fields, farmland, pasture and woods. Corn was parceled everywhere and you saw the restful countryside scattered with houses and bungalows and displays of nurseries, markets, stores and churches and other sources supplying life. The area offered celebrations and activities that included: "Dover Days"; "Punkin' Chunkin"; "Apple Scrapple"; "The Fifer Peach Festival" "The State Fair", "Harness Racing" and a tremendous "May Day" celebration."

Tears coursed down her face as Anita read the final statement in his book, an anthology on the topic of artists and on writers in particular:

"A writer has been given the gift to channel the universe, the dark depths circling life, love, reality, everyone and everything. In other words, a writer's job is to describe the subtle, silent places, the stored away magic and mystery calling him or her to empty into the dark, forlorn forest…the space of the heart and mind, the life capsule. The writer possesses a plaintive song, a dream of aspiration, consolation, knowledge, inspiration and optimism to interpret, and pour into a world culture. Writers have a purpose to energetically use every stretch of the imagination, and be disciplined as they engage the flow of creativity circling life."

THE END